Harriet, I
I'm glad I n
you. Things do g
better. Best wishes,
Anita

DIVORCE RECOVERY

Piecing Together Your Broken Dreams

DIVORCE RECOVERY

Piecing Together Your Broken Dreams

ANITA BROCK
and the Divorce Recovery Team

WORTHY
PUBLISHING
FORT WORTH, TEXAS

Unless otherwise noted, scripture quotations are from the *Holy Bible: New International Version* (NIV), copyright © 1978 by the International Bible Society. Used by permission of Zondervan Bible Publishers.

Copyright © 1988 by Worthy Publishing, Fort Worth, Texas 76137.

Library of Congress Catalog Card Number 87-43328

ISBN 0-8344-0166-5

10 9 8 7 6 5 4 3 2 1

Dedication

This book is dedicated to my mother, Doris Massie, and my singles' minister, Mike Washburn, both of whom have been my own personal cheerleaders.

Did they stumble so as to fall beyond recovery? Not at all!

Romans 11:11

Acknowledgments

A good editor is a beloved person. Mary Hollingsworth, my editor, qualifies as a good editor. She has tactfully done her work with me during lunch breaks, early morning breakfasts, weekends, business hours and off-duty hours. I love her dearly and am grateful to know her.

I am also grateful to the many people who have opened their hearts and lives in the divorce recovery class. My life has been blessed by seeing people rise from the low point in their lives to heights unforeseen through the discussion classes we have in this ministry. They make this work worthwhile and rewarding, and their experiences sprinkle the entirety of this book. I love each one with a special compassion.

The cofacilitators I have worked with deserve a special thanks. Tedd Massie, Bill Evans, Melva Evans, Janet Ashlocke-Steele and Randy Shantz have all cried with the crying, rejoiced with the rejoicing and have been dedicated to this work and to each other in carrying out this work. We have been a family-team with a unified vision of serving God and the divorced. We have loved and supported each other through many trials during the growth and development of divorce recovery classes. They all have helped me learn and organize materials, and together we have prayed about and discussed the divorce process. They even continued to love me while I marched to a different drummer during my absorption in the writing of this book.

Mike Washburn, my minister, has been very special during this process also. He critiqued the manuscript, offered advice and encouraged me in many ways. He has shared my excitement and anxiety during this year of book writing, as well as during the preceding years of involvement in the divorce recovery program. And, of course, he has developed the Leader's Guide for this book.

A really special thanks goes to Randy Shantz. He has been a dear friend and an encouragement. He listened to my fears and joys about this project; he reminded me of incidents I had forgotten; he loaned me his typewriter; he let me bounce ideas off him; he gave me feedback, advice and comfort. I am really grateful to him for giving me the inspiration and freedom to dream. He has been a landmark in my life and in the writing of this book. Because he has been so special in the divorce recovery ministry and to me, I must acknowledge his special contribution to the writing of this book: Randy numbered the pages!

Thanks,

Anita Brock

Table of Contents

Introduction

The divorce recovery *program* is about newness of life. It is a gentle, small group therapy program to help people hurting from the devastation and sin surrounding divorce to get on the road to emotional recovery and to realize the wonderful grace of God that encompasses all of his precious children — single, married or single-again.

This book is *not* a discussion of the right or wrong of divorce. Divorce should be avoided at every turn. The Bible is clear on this point. And we affirm that truth.

The question is, when divorce has been thrust upon someone, when divorce has not been avoided, a marriage has been ripped apart and dreams have been broken, then what? Should the bleeding, wounded victims be left on the side of the road to die as the church walks piously by on the other side as the priest and Levite did? Or should we respond with loving compassion by lifting the crushed and broken person onto our donkey and leading him down the road to recovery? What would the Savior do?

That's what this book is about — recovery. It doesn't offer quick fixes, because there aren't any. It offers practical, realistic suggestions of proven, workable steps toward recovery. It offers hope and real help. And with it comes my prayer for your full recovery and return to your life's dreams through the grace of God.

Anita

P.S.
The stories of people in this book are basically true. However, to protect the privacy of these hurting people, names have been changed, and some incidents have been adapted or altered slightly. We trust you will find help and healing through the recovering experiences related by these wonderful folks.

1

A Roller Coaster Ride

S ome vacation," I thought as I stood before the mirror looking at a week's growth of beard and red, blood-shot eyes. "This week has not turned out like I thought it would."

I had thought I could make the hurt go away in a week. When the divorce was granted, I took a week's vacation to get myself together again. The year of separation had been dreadful, but the day in court left me drained, exhausted of all energy. I couldn't go back to work yet. I had to get my emotions under control and revitalize myself.

My plan failed me. I thought I was going to die. I locked myself in the apartment. I wouldn't answer the phone, read the mail or see anyone. To ease my misery, I stocked up on booze, more booze than I had ever seen at one time. I spent the week drinking and crying. After seventeen years of marriage, my life had been wiped out in one day with the crash of the gavel and the echoing words, "Divorce granted."

THE UNREAL WORLD

During the separation I was barely functional. I was living in an unreal world. I couldn't believe this was happening to me. I kept waiting for the nightmare to end. My life was in a state of limbo I kept thinking. I went to work each day and couldn't remember on the way home if I had done my work. Since I didn't get fired, I assume I did the work.

For the last year, after the work day, when I would walk into the apartment, sometimes I noticed the mess.

Most times I didn't. When the dresser drawers were empty of clean socks and underwear, I would look around and notice the mess. Pizza cartons. Soft drink cans. Dirty clothes everywhere. Mail stacked up.

"How could she do this to me?" I questioned over and over. "It isn't fair. I deserve better than this." But nothing happened to make it better. She didn't come back.

When the divorce was final, hard reality began to sink in, but I couldn't face it. I just couldn't believe this was actually the end of my marriage. It felt like the end of the world, as if I had lived for nothing. So I took a week's vacation to pull myself together, but my life was too out of control. Order still didn't come.

During my week of self-imposed lock-in, I thought about this past year. It had been a year of nothingness, and it had been everything. I was numb, feeling nothingness as I drove around the loop of the city many nights, and as many as four times in a night, trying to think. I thought about what went wrong, what I should have done, how I could get even, and what I would say the next time I saw her. I even thought, "What if we get back together?"

During my state of limbo, I didn't pay the bills. The money was there, I was still working, but it wasn't my job. She had always paid the bills. After the electricity was cut off, I paid the bills . . . but life was still empty and aimless.

When "D" day came, I thought the vacation plan was the answer, that time itself was the solution. I didn't use the time well though. I just became more numb as the beer cans thrown in the corner piled higher, and the stink become ranker. I stayed in the apartment and cried and drank. Then I cried *because* I was drinking. I had never been a drinking man.

I thought I was going crazy. I have always thought of myself as a family man, a working man. I was a stable, church-going Rock of Gibraltar. So what is happening? Am I losing my mind?

PLAN B

When I looked at myself in the mirror, I didn't like what I saw. I leaned in toward the mirror and began talking to myself.

"James, you have sunk as low as you can go. You need to get hold of yourself. Pull yourself up! Sure, you didn't want life to turn out this way, but you're making it worse, not better. Right now you're such a low worm, you deserve to get stepped on and squashed. You've got to develop a Plan B."

Plan B for James was to attend the divorce recovery discussion group at a nearby church. He sat in class thankful for the opportunity to work through his pain by expressing it with friends who understood and accepted him and his story. Being able to express his hurt in a supportive setting was far more productive than his lock-in had been. Plan B helped him deal with his pain, not just feel it over and over.

He told the group that after his talk to himself in the mirror, he began the alternate plan with a shower and a shave. Then he got a shovel and garbage bags and began to clean up his apartment. He paid his bills and fixed himself a decent dinner. As his apartment cleared, his mind began to clear. He began to think about what to do next. He began to see a semblance of order to his chaotic emotions.

James took the next step in his Plan B. He went back to the church and began developing friendships that would be uplifting, not defeating. He found the divorce recovery class receptive to him and his problems.

In class he talked about his pain, his anger and his mixed emotions. He loved her and hated her and sometimes felt compassion for her. Sometimes he hated himself, sometimes loved himself, sometimes felt compassion for himself. His compassion for others certainly grew stronger as he listened to their stories in class. He understood their trauma, and they understood his, because it was trauma they shared through similar experiences.

Through the following weeks James got a handle on his life again. And he began making the necessary changes toward renewed stability. He never said the change was easy, only that it was necessary and worthwhile.

After hearing James' story, others in class began to open up, too. "Like you, James, I thought in the beginning, 'This is not real; this can't be happening to me, not ME, Lord.' It has been difficult to face reality. I didn't want what was real. I wanted what I had, or what I thought I had."

THE PROCESS OF DIVORCE

James had struggled through the process of divorce. And it *is* a process — one that everyone experiencing divorce must go through in order to reach healing. It's like a long, dark tunnel through which you grope, unable to see or get your bearings, until finally a tiny light appears at the far end. When you see the light, then you stumble forward and start to run until you burst out into the sunshine at the far end. You know you've made it. Life is *not* over. Yes, the dreams are broken, but a new life is there for the taking.

What is the process? How can you know you're in the process and how far along you are? When will the light appear to give you hope? Consider these steps in the process.

The Denial Dilemma

Denial is a universal reaction to divorce, as well as to other types of loss. Many men and women going through divorce are shocked at this turn of events in their lives. The one who initiates the divorce went through a period of denial *before* making the decision, a period of denying while wrestling with the decision. Even after divorce is initiated, both parties use denial as a coping mechanism against the turmoil. This method is helpful and healthy, but only for a while. Denial is a stall, a biding of time to gain the strength for facing reality.

Jane had suspected that her husband had been fondling their daughter, but she could not think of a solution. She kept denying the evidence because the reality was too overwhelming, but subconsciously she was seeking answers to her dilemma. She began to realize she needed professional help. She began to realize the living arrangement had to change. Only when answers began to emerge was she able to quit denying, act on some solutions and make the decisions necessary for ending this horrendous situation. That decision had to be divorce.

James and Jane were able to quit saying, "This is not happening to me," as they grew emotionally stronger and found the needed solutions to their problems.

The Thrill of Transition

When divorcing people move out of the dilemma of denial, the transition to singleness and reality really begins. The transition from married to single is like a roller coaster ride — unpredictable: some thrilling highs, devastating lows, surprises, quick turns, wild- 'n-scary, breathtaking experiences. But, like a roller coaster, transition eventually slows down, stabilizes and can even be renewing. Getting off the roller coaster onto steady ground feels good.

Remaining Roles

While on this roller coaster of transition, one of the first challenges is the feeling of loss because an important role has been lost, the role of wife/husband. Some claim this loss of role leaves them feeling like a half-person, an incomplete person.

In marriage one life meshes with another, and interdependency prevails. Two become one. Often the roles are definite and defined. In divorce the mesh is shattered, the interdependency is broken, definition of roles seems to be lacking. But what is left is not two half-people; it's two "whole" people.

Look at the roles you performed in marriage: wife/ husband, brother/sister, mother/dad, neighbor, friend, teacher, servant, worker, housekeeper, nursemaid, cook, entertainer and many more. Which of these roles are lost due to divorce? Only one — the wife/husband role. Since the combined roles you perform make up the total you, and all but one role remain, that does not reduce you to a half person. What remains is you, a whole person with the loss of only one role.

It reminds me of a team of two perfectly matched thoroughbreds pulling a carriage together. If one thoroughbred is unhitched from the carriage, the other one doesn't turn into a mule — he's still a thoroughbred. It may be a little more difficult to pull the carriage alone, but he can do it, because he's still a thoroughbred.

Hopeless Hanging On

It's true that the loss of this important role is significant to your personal life. This loss affects your stability, your well being, even your identity, for a while. Replacing this loss constitutes transition, and change is frightening in the beginning.

This fear of change keeps people hanging on, clinging to a false security because of the uncertain paths which lie ahead and the new roles that emerge.

Carla said, "I have been alone for a year now. I would rather be unhappy married than unhappy single." She could not make a decision. She was immobile, wringing her hands and trembling. Because of fear, because the change was too emotional, Carla was trying to hang on to a marriage that was self-destructive and nonexistent. The new roles were frightening, the transition too challenging. She couldn't see beyond her tears. The more she talked, the more she could see the sense of letting go and moving on. She had thought nobody would understand her uncertainty, but as she talked, her listeners did understand, and she began to gain trust in her ability to move on.

Hanging on is an understandable stage, but it's a stage that must be replaced with letting go and moving on. It's like staying in a boat that's headed over the waterfall. You can hang on to keep from rocking the boat and eventually crash on the rocks below, or you can let go, jump out and swim to safety. Sure, you'll rock the boat when you jump, but at least you won't drown!

To get in control of life again, you need understanding, assurance, support and feelings of normalcy. Knowing that others have felt the same fears and uncertainties helps.

DIVORCE MYTHOLOGY

The Greeks didn't have a corner on the market for myths. People involved in the process of divorce have their own paranoid mythology that plagues their minds and emotions during this turbulent time. The only comfort is to remember that they are, in fact, *myths*, not truths. Do you recognize any of these feelings of paranoia?

Myth 1: "Nobody Understands"

An uncertainty that Carla and others express is, "Nobody knows the troubles I've seen." Carla's belief that nobody understands her situation is one of the common myths regarding divorce. Everyone's life and divorce situation is unique. It's so unique, in fact, that understanding seems totally out of the question. The fact is, though, other divorced people *do* understand. They understand the out-of- control emotions, the incredible hurt, the hand-wringing anguish and the white-hot anger. They may not understand the specific details, but they can identify with the emotions. And all people, divorced or not, can understand pain.

Myth 2: "I Am Going to Die"

Pain is what is expressed when someone says, "I am going to die," which is another common myth about divorce expressed by James. It is common for those going through divorce to think this is the literal end of life. The truth is, nobody ever died from a disease called *divorce*. Hurt a great deal? Yes. Wish you were dead? Yes. Die? No.

Myth 3: "Everybody Is Looking at Me"

"Everybody is looking at me," is a paranoid utterance of the divorced which is also untrue. Jim put it more bluntly when he said, "I feel like I have the scarlet letter D stamped on my forehead." Because of increased emotional sensitivity during divorce, people become SELF conscious. As a rule, though, outer appearance does not change so much that people stare. It is true that in divorce some people lose weight, some gain weight, some get circles under their eyes and, although this is noticeable, people on the street don't stop and whisper, "There goes a divorcee." Probably only your closest friends and family will notice any change.

Myth 4: "Everybody Hates Me — God Hates Me"

Maybe it is true that birds of a feather think alike. It is true that people with common experiences come up with common ideas about the experiences, and these ideas emerge individually. "Everybody hates me — God hates me" is another common idea of divorcees. However, everybody does not hate you. Some will relate to you differently because of *their* self-consciousness. Some friends drift away because of their insecurities. Most people do not know what to say and would appreciate your help in finding a way to relate to you that is new or different. Some, unfortunately, don't care — they just don't give a flip.

God *does* care. God hates divorce, but he loves his divorced child. God hates sin, but he loves the sinner. So another myth bites the dust.

Knowing these myths is helpful. It helps to know that others have had the same insane thoughts you've had. Also it helps to be assured that a few insane thoughts do not make an insane person. Insane thoughts are generally temporary. They come from the sudden surge of emotions. Thankfully, the brain does usually take over again, and the insane thoughts and behaviors become a part of the past.

Unfortunately, this is not true of everyone who faces divorce. Some people, who do not begin the difficult road to recovery allow their temporary insanity to become permanent. Some who do not begin to get control of their emotions and reign in their lives "go over the edge" to emotional breakdown. Some even give up life entirely and commit suicide rather than struggle with self through to a healthy recovery.

Professional counseling during these stormy times is invaluable. A good counselor can be the anchor to life and sanity that you need. It's like seeing an optometrist when your eyesight is weak or a doctor when you've got the flu. Counselors are physicians of the mind and emotions. A good counselor is likely the one who can get you started on the road to recovery. And while this book is built around a group therapy model, you may also want to consider seeing a qualified professional for your own specific struggles.

As the divorce process proceeds, the transition becomes easier. Reality becomes easier to face as you deal with the pain and the negative emotions, as we will do in the following chapters.

James discovered that honest expression helped him put his pain in the past. He had to reckon with his past in order to have hope for his future. Understanding he was not alone or crazy was the first step toward regaining control and putting his life in order again.

Divorce Recovery Journal

Your first step in regaining control of your life is to begin your divorce recovery journal. Take a spiral notebook, legal pad or notebook paper. Begin by writing a response to James. Write him a letter, or a note. Say anything you want. He won't see it. Nobody will. Nobody cares about spelling or handwriting. It is your journal.

After writing him a note, write paragraphs on the two topics listed below. When you finish this book and your journal, you can go back and read your entries. You will see a difference in you. This journal will be your measure of transition and growth. You will see a renewed you. Reality is acceptable, and transition to a better life is possible. The healing of your wounds is desirable, is within reach and within you.

1. My biggest struggle right now is . . .
2. The thing that really gets me down is . . .

The Un-Merry-Go-Round

I've been mad too long. My anger has been building and building. For at least two years before the divorce, I became aware of my anger. My mother took a picture of my husband and me one Sunday afternoon a couple of years ago, before the divorce, on the front porch of her house. When the picture came back, I was shocked to see the contradiction the picture showed. I was smiling, my face looked pleasant enough, but my hand was in such a tight fist that even in the picture, I could see the veins in my hand stand out. I looked at that picture a long time and thought, 'There stands an angry woman. Look at that fist.' Yet, my face didn't seem to show the same feeling. I've thought about that picture a lot since then."

EXPLOSIVE ANGER

"My divorce was final five months ago, but I'm still as angry today as I've ever been. I know I can't continue this way. I can't live with this much anger. I'm like a time bomb with only a few seconds left before I blow up.

"This anger makes me act in ways that aren't really me. The other day I went through my mail and saw an ad from Acme Wholesale Furniture for a sale that had ended the day before. It was addressed to Preferred Customer. At first I just chuckled, thinking, 'How preferred am I? I got the ad a day late.' Then I began to stew about it. Who does Acme Wholesale Furniture think they are to try and fool everyone into thinking they are preferred. They must think I'm some dummy to believe I'm preferred when they don't even bother to get the ad to me on time. The more I thought about it, the madder I got. The madder I got, the more I wanted to tell them just what I thought of their crummy ad and their phony Preferred Customer list.

"Finally, I called the store and asked for the manager. He came to the phone, and I let him have it. I told him I got this ad the day after the sale, and I was mad. If I was so 'preferred,' why hadn't I been notified earlier of the sale? I told him I was buying a new house because I was divorced now, and I wanted all new furniture, but I was not buying from them because of the way they treated me. He was very apologetic and said to come on in and they would honor the same prices on anything I wanted. I told him I would not buy from them ever, I would always remember the way they had treated me, and I would tell all my friends not to buy from them either. I was awful . . . I'm not getting a new house. I'm not getting new furniture. I *am* divorced. That's the only truth I told.

"I know it's the anger over my divorce that made me make such a fool of myself with the furniture store manager. I'd be embarrassed to go in there now. I have got to do something about this anger before I make a fool of myself all over town."

Marianne was soft spoken as she said this in the small group discussion at a seminar. She had a timid manner about her; she appeared to be calm, poised and gentle, but . . . Marianne was struggling. She was struggling with her strong emotions because her strong emotions were controlling her.

Someone at the table asked her what she had ever done to vent her anger besides call the furniture store manager.

She replied, "I suppose pictures are important to me. After the divorce I took all the 8 x 10 wedding pictures and tacked them to a tree out back. Then I took my handgun and shot every picture. Not just once, but I shot each one many times, until there was nothing left of the picture. I had thought this would cure all anger. It helped, but only for a short time. I need a long-time cure."

This was certainly an explosive way of dealing with anger.

Actually Marianne had taken the first steps in resolving her anger. She recognized it and was beginning to understand it. At least she was beginning to understand how it affected her behavior. She also realized that her anger was the long-lasting reaction to the downfall of her marriage.

RESOLVING ANGER

Many people do not recognize anger in themselves. Children are so conditioned not to show temper, to be patient, to be sweet, that they grow into adults thinking anger is wrong; therefore, the outcome is to suppress or deny honest anger. When the anger is suppressed, it becomes resentment, bitterness or depression.

Suppressing or stuffing the anger creates more problems, rather than solving any problems. Recognizing the anger and admitting it is the first step in resolving it.

Then comes the need to understand anger. You need to understand what it is and what it will do to you. By understanding anger more, the solutions become easier and the anger becomes more controllable.

A SECONDARY EMOTION

First is the need to understand that anger is a secondary emotion, a response to another emotion, such as fear, hurt or frustration. To better understand the anger, look at the emotion behind it and deal with that emotion.

Frustration

For instance, to deal with the emotion of frustration, recognize that the good life is not a life free of frustration, but a life of bounce-back ability.

In discussing his divorce, Roy said, "I get so frustrated because nothing goes my way anymore. I used to be the decision maker, the head of a household. Now decisions are made without me."

Darian asked him, "Are the decisions made without you disastrous?"

"No," Roy answered. "Sometimes the decisions are the same as I would have made."

"Do the decisions made without you affect you greatly?" Darian asked him.

"No, not really. My ex-wife changed jobs. That was a major decision that did not affect me at all, yet I felt slighted that we hadn't talked about it. I am also thinking of the decisions about our son. My ex-wife discusses what I call major issues with me, but I want to still be involved in minor issues, too."

Darian thought a minute and said, "Rather than be distressed with frustration, why don't you just say to yourself, 'So What?' Since there is no pending disaster, and it doesn't make much difference any way, I get away from a lot of frustration with a 'So What?' attitude."

"I hadn't thought about it that way," Roy replied, and he agreed a change in attitude could help. A change in attitude is called for when the circumstances cannot be changed. An increase in tolerance gets rid of many frustrations and its following anger.

Fear

Fears behind anger also require a change in attitude. Fears are such nonsense. They are certainly real, but still nonsense. Fear of the future, fear of the unknown, fear of disaster — all these fears can be crippling to the happy life.

These fears are unnecessary. Nearly always the fears are irrational, yet they have a far reaching effect.

Just about everyone has a fear of snakes, yet most people live their whole life and never meet up with a live snake. Further, of all the snakes in the world, only a small percent are poisonous. So, fear of snakes is usually irrational. Life's fear is like the fear of snakes. You probably won't meet up with most of them head on, and most of them aren't poisonous anyway.

Florence said, "Fear kept me in a marriage much longer than I should have been. I was afraid of my husband, but I was afraid to leave, too. Life was a no-win situation for me. Whatever I did, I was afraid."

A change in perspective can remove many fears, especially if the fearful person is questioned about how threatening the fear is anyway. Irrational fears can be conquered with rational thinking, and the anger coming from the fear can be lessened.

Pain

Pain is never pleasant, and nobody intentionally experiences pain, unless there is a more long-range benefit. Sometimes, though, pain facilitates healing. For instance, surgery is painful, but if it successfully eliminates cancer, then the temporary pain is worthwhile in the long run.

Anger causes pain, but the pain experienced from anger can be lessened. The pain is real and there is usually reason for it, but not forever. One way of lessening the pain is to share it. When pain is shared, it is cut in half.

Karen cried quietly for an hour one evening, listening to others talk. Finally she said, "I hurt so much. I can't quit hurting. I don't always know why I hurt so much, but I always feel it. Maybe it's over my lost dreams."

Others were touched by her tears and identified with the hurt over lost dreams. After about fifteen minutes of discussion with her, Karen said, "When I hurt so much, I really do feel better after I talk to someone. I go over to my mother's sometimes and cry on her shoulder, and then I go home feeling better. I haven't been a crier all my life. Be patient with me. I know someday I won't cry all the time."

Karen cried and talked and shared her pain in following weeks, and her pain did eventually become manageable. By crying and talking she was dealing with the emotion behind her anger, and her anger became manageable, too.

Karen learned that her anger was a demand. Respect had been missing in her marriage. As she dealt with her pain, she began to understand that her anger was a demand for her to be respected.

ANGER IS DEMANDS

To further understand anger, you must also understand that anger is a demand — a demand to be heard, to be understood and to be respected. You can meet these demands more easily without anger.

For instance, if no one is listening to you, look at the way you are presenting what you are saying. To be heard maybe your voice needs to be softened, or the words may need to be less harsh and critical. An attacking expression of anger is usually tuned out.

The feeling of not being understood comes from within. Truthfully, people do understand anger and pain, for it is common to all. Again, listen to your manner of speaking to develop the skill of expressing for understanding. Watch how others get their understanding and learn from your observation. People want to understand. Give them gentle words with which to work, and they will.

When you honestly express yourself, you will increase understanding. Begin statements with, "I feel like . . ." Then take an honest, deep look at how you will complete the sentence. This increases your understanding and enables others to understand also.

Anger that demands respect defeats its own purpose. Respect is earned by respectful behavior. Self-respect gathers momentum from the respect of others. A person looking up to a standard of respect is looked up to by others. These demands can be met without demanding behavior. The angry heart actually prevents the meeting of these demands.

Actually, anger prevents your reaching many of your goals in life. It prevents problem solving, it prevents constructive communication and it prevents friendships.

I have a dear friend, Frances Shinn, who tells me that the first time she saw me she was afraid to ask, "How are you?" for fear I would answer, because I looked so angry. The next time she saw me she spoke anyway, because that's the kind of person she is. I gradually resolved my anger, and we developed a close friendship. But if I hadn't, I would have missed a wonderful friend. No one seeks out an angry friend.

Brad said one night, "I don't blame her for not coming back. I wouldn't want to live with someone as angry as me either. I am going to do something about this anger of mine. If I only knew what to do."

HANDLING ANGER

What can be done with anger? Here are three suggestions:

1. Use the energy anger generates to pull away when necessary, to stand up when necessary, to knock

down walls and establish communication. Some of the most productive communication follows the statement, "This makes me mad." Such honest expression knocks down walls that prevent communication and helps clear the air for understanding. When ventilated with "I feel . . ." expressions instead of "You did . . ." expressions, honest understanding can follow.

2. Walk and talk theory: Exercise, such as walking or bicycling, burns up the energy that might turn into an explosion otherwise. After exercise, calmer talk may be possible. Talk that is not attacking helps resolve anger.

3. Accept the *feeling* of anger as normal; recognize that it's the *acting out* of anger that is not acceptable.

Hunger for Vengeance

Acting out anger happens so often in the divorce process. It is called hunger for vengeance. People who have not gone through a divorce cannot understand the temporary insanity behind vengeance. People who have gone through divorce know exactly the temporary insanity that goes with that desire to get even with the one that has hurt you.

People seek revenge when they've been humiliated. A slight hurt doesn't call for revenge, but humiliation damages the self-esteem and demands response. Often divorce is humiliating. The other person has put you down, and you think revenge will restore your lost honor. Not so. This kind of thinking actually puts the other person in control of your honor.

Slashing someone's tires does not restore your honor; such an act of immaturity only further removes your honor. Visualize a pretty lady in a respectable-looking suit, high-heeled shoes, groomed hair, painted fingernails, out in the dark of night with a machete slashing tires. Would you describe her as honorable? Probably not.

A HUNDRED WAYS TO GET EVEN

Al shared his memories of vengeance in class one evening. "One night I couldn't sleep. I remembered being told that writing down your thoughts helped get a handle on runaway emotions. So I began to write. I listed 100 ways to get even with my ex that wouldn't get me thrown in jail.

"Some of the ways were very clever and made me laugh to think of them. I thought about stealing road signs and putting them in her yard while she was out on a date. Such signs as: Men Working, Detour, Yield, Dangerous Crossing and Watch Out for Children. Wouldn't that impress her date?

"Others I listed were mean, such as pouring concrete in her azalea bed or pouring a can of motor oil in her driveway.

"I didn't carry out these threats, but I felt better for just listing them. I went back to bed and slept. The next morning I looked at the list, and it looked silly. It reminded me of high school pranks."

Others have not dismissed vengeance so easily. There are some true stories about vengeance. Some even make the newspaper. I read about a man who went to the home of his estranged wife with a shotgun and shot her bed over and over. I really don't want to go that crazy.

As a rule, temporary insanity is kept temporary. Some tires have been slashed, some midnight oil burned, some late night phone calls have been made. But honor was not restored. These acts did not make the humiliation go away.

LIVING WELL, LOOKING WELL

Marsha gave a delightful story about vengeance to the group in discussion one evening. She said, "When Matt and I separated I was so depressed I couldn't get out of bed many days. I couldn't leave the house, even to buy groceries. I couldn't drive, I couldn't even watch TV. I have never had anything make me feel so down. And I looked awful — swollen eyes, blotched face, messy hair.

"To make things worse, he was having a good time with his new girlfriend, or so I imagined. I really wanted to get even. I really wanted him to suffer.

"My neighbor would not leave me alone. She kept reaching out to me, even though I didn't want her to. I was rude to her many times, but she didn't give up. Eventually, I started talking, and she listened. Gradually, I began to adjust and come out of my shell. In a few months I was really feeling worthwhile again. One afternoon I spruced up and went to the mall.

"Lo and behold, I faced Matt at a check stand. He looked awful. His clothes were frumpy, he wasn't as well groomed as I remembered. His affair had not lasted long, he said. He looked tired and sad. He said he was lonely and had missed me far more than he had expected.

"Then he began to really look at me. He kept saying, 'You really look nice. You are looking good.' I couldn't say the same for him. When I turned to leave, he said, 'How have you adjusted so well? I am really envious of how well you are doing while I am doing so poorly.'

"I remembered the agony I had gone through, and I was glad I was better. I remembered how I had wanted him to suffer. I remembered how I had wanted to get even. Now I had. I stood there thinking, 'This is my sweet moment, and I wasn't even looking for it.' Now I can testify that living well and looking well are the best vengeance I could have."

Before you seek revenge, ask yourself what you have contributed to the situation. People seek revenge because they are not owning up to their part. Denying your part and harming the other person for your hurt does not improve the situation. Wait. What goes around comes around. As Marsha learned, living well and looking well are the best vengeance.

FIRST AID TECHNIQUES

The pain you feel is such a bummer, living well has to replace it. Only so much suffering can be tolerated till first aid is necessary.

The Healing Touch of Time

One first aid measure is to trust time. Lessons are learned, and conclusions are drawn over periods of time. Life becomes manageable again as you are forced to try new ways of acting, new ways of feeling and thinking as a single. The pain urges you to the kind of action that heals and changes.

When the body is in pain, fever burns off the impurities. With emotional pain, impurities must also be burned off. Pain motivates the necessary action, the fever, to remove the suffering.

The Un-Merry-Go-Round

Emotional pain is devastating, it leads to self-destruction, which adds more disaster, and thus more pain. To ease the pain, people seeking relief often self-destruct through gambling, eating disorders, promiscuity, drinking, overspending. This postpones the pain and brings on guilt, anger and fear. Then, in an attempt to hide the guilt, anger or fear, they withdraw so that nobody will know. The withdrawal creates isolation from other people. The isolation is lonely, and nobody likes loneliness. So the pain becomes greater.

This pain cycle is like riding a merry-go-round that is stuck. You go to the amusement park and get on the ride thinking it will be fun, but then it gets stuck. You're going up and down, and around and around at the same time. The speed picks up, and the music gets louder. The motion makes you dizzy and even nauseated. The merry-go-round doesn't quit, and the cycle gets faster and faster. The amusement becomes monstrous.

Stop the Cycle

What can you do with this pain? How can you short circuit the pain cycle and get off the merry-go-round? Try these:

1. *Turn it over to someone else.* It's too much to bear alone. Admit it, and talk it out with someone you can trust, such as a counselor.

2. *Cry it out.* Cry for the losses and the hurt. Tears are a healing mechanism the good Lord gave us. You will get tired of crying as the proper amount of grieving takes place, and you'll move into the next stage.

3. *Make a grieving date.* Set aside a time to deal with the pain, like Saturday morning, 9:00 to 11:00. Determine that you will devote two hours, or whatever you need, to the pain. Concentrate on the pain. Bring up all the painful memories. Let nothing distract or interfere with feeling the pain.

When the time is up, go on to something else, knowing that you can give yourself another pain session later if it's necessary. The times needed will become less often and shorter.

4. *Throw it away.* Take scraps of paper and label them with your pains. For instance, write "Pain of rejection," "Pain of not having custody," "Pain of guilt." Think about each one. Then throw the papers in the trash. Fill up the trash can with your discarded pain.

Conclusion

Marianne's anger, Roy's frustration and Karen's pain are typical reactions to divorce. Everyone has felt these emotions at some time. These emotions and life in general can be brought back into control again. The merry-go-round can be stopped. As you come to terms with the past, the emotions of the present become less hurtful.

Divorce Recovery Journal

To help get the negative emotions resolved and put to rest, pick up your divorce recovery journal and begin to write about your own thoughts regarding anger, vengeance and pain.

Especially complete the following sentences in your own words in your journal:

1. I get angry when . . .

2. Next time I am angry, I want to try . . .

3. The thing that really hurts is . . .

4. What I really want is . . .

All Hung Up

*H*aving a flat tire can be devastating, even when you know how to fix it. It keeps you from getting on down the road. It keeps you from going where you want to go. At least for a brief moment it makes you feel helpless. It's unexpected and always inconvenient.

What do you do when you have a flat tire? Do you kick it? Do you kick the other tires? Do you throw away the whole car because one tire is flat? Do you decide that all cars of this model are bad because yours has a flat? Probably not.

Emotional hang ups are like flat tires. These hang ups keep you from getting on down the road, from getting where you want to go. These hang ups may make you helpless for a time. They certainly are inconvenient to your growth and sense of well-being.

What do you do with your emotional hang ups? Do you kick yourself with it? Do you whip others with it? Do you throw away your whole life? Hopefully not.

The flat tires in life are not major, but they are influential. These flat tires, or hang ups, are common to everyone, including divorcees. Like flat tires, the sensible thing to do is remove the hang-up and fix it. Then get rolling again.

HANG UPS

Generalizing

One of the emotional hang ups that is common to the divorcee is that of overgeneralizing.

You overgeneralize when you take one or two beliefs and, without examining them, make them apply to life in general. Our teenagers do this when they say, "Everybody stays out all night on prom night." They are generalizing from a small amount of knowledge and trying to make it a worldwide acceptable action.

Divorcees often do this by generalizing, "All women are loose," "No man can be trusted," "All women think about is money," "All redheads are temperamental" or "My situation is the worst." These statements say more about the speaker than about the topic. They express the speaker's failure to examine the facts. The statements also say, "They are flawed; I am flawless," which is another unwarranted generalization.

To get away from this trap, drop the flag words "always" and "never." Replace them with more accurate words, such as "sometimes," "may," "often" or "it seems to me." By doing this, you decrease your own fears, feelings of disgust or guilt, which go along with this emotional hang up.

Self-fulfilling Prophecy

Another common flat tire heard among divorcees is the self-fulfilling prophecy.

Meg repeatedly made the statement, "I'll never find anyone else," after her divorce. Of course, she won't either. Her self-fulfilling prophecy defeated her. She couldn't see the people around her for being blinded by her prophecy. Her prophecy also gave her a defeated attitude and look. She won't find anyone with that defeated look on her face.

Joe and Danya had been dating a long time. They appeared to have a workable relationship, but Joe kept saying, "It won't work with us." His self-fulfilling prophecy said more about where he was coming from than about where he was going.

Self-fulfilling prophecies undermine your relationships. To fix this flat, determine ahead of time to make it work, not make it fail. Decide to meet others, rather than deciding you won't. Your "vibes" show, your prophecies can come true. "As a man thinketh in his heart, so is he" (Proverbs 23:7, *KJV*).

Therefore, control of the prophecies is necessary in order to get away from a self-defeating emotional hang up.

Unreal Expectations

Unreal expectations is another trap used to justify a miserable life. You set an unreal expectation, such as, "Everyone who loves me will always be on time to show proper consideration for my feelings." Invariably, someone will be late. Then you can say, "See, nobody loves me." This then justifies a state of misery and becomes an emotional trap.

To get out of this trap, develop flexibilities in your expectations that will allow exceptions and special consideration. Avoid words such as "should" and "must." To say, "I should be happy now" forces you to make unhealthy demands on yourself. Actually taking steps in that direction is far healthier. Bitter disappointment follows unreal expectations, making two flat tires instead of one.

Guy erroneously thought a new sports car would make him popular. He admitted his mistake when he said, "I have never been friendly. I called it not being a good mixer. That didn't sting so much. I decided a Jaguar was what I needed to be a better mixer. In a roundabout way it worked. My excitement over this ambition helped me to talk more and be friendlier. You know what? My thinking was wrong, and my expectations were unreal when I thought the car would make the difference. The truth is, I make the difference."

Murphy's Law

Murphy's Law states that if anything bad can happen, it will; if anything *can* go wrong, it will. This is another hang up divorcees often have.

Before going to court, Teri was sick with anxiety. "He said when we get to court he will prove me an unfit mother. He said he knows ways to convince the judge. I have always been a good mother, but he has always been a slick talker. I don't know what will happen. I don't know what he's going to say. I won't know how to defend myself. I can't think of anything he could accuse me of. I'm just going to die when I get there. I will be tongue-tied, I will stutter. They will listen to him. The worst is going to happen."

Teri was out of touch with reality. The worst is not always going to happen.

After his divorce, Roger kept saying, "My business will fail now. She always kept my books. I'm not going to survive this."

His statement exemplifies unreal expectations, self-fulfilling prophecy and Murphy's Law. Roger needs to fix his flats by realizing that almost everyone survives and that he is defeating himself with this approach.

Doubting your ability to survive heightens your anxiety level and prevents constructive problem solving. Murphy's Law says things are bad and getting worse, disaster is right around the corner. This outlook of future disaster makes the present more anxious, too.

Give up Murphy's Law. Instead, think of the probability percentage. Are the chances of pending disaster .01 percent, .1 percent or 1 percent? When the worry comes up, write down its rating of probability. Then 24 hours later write down the probability it appears to have then. It will likely be lower. Seeing a pending disaster as probable one day and unlikely the next helps depower the disaster.

Wallowing

Wallowing is an emotional trap that divorcees experience. Wallowing is the "pity party," the indulgence of self-pity. Withdrawing for a time of grieving is okay and necessary, but living there after a year or two is too much. That is enjoying misery. Although misery loves company, there won't be much company, because company doesn't love misery.

At a singles' retreat Sandy was telling her group how lonely she had been since her divorce. "I don't get invited over to friends' dinners or parties anymore, and I am so miserable without him that I often make up excuses to call just so I can talk to him."

She let the tears flow as she talked. Everyone could feel her pain and loneliness.

"I feel so bad that we divorced. The kids were only 12 and 14 at the time. I really feel sorry for them, growing up without their father, and he was such a good father."

Deidra responded to Sandy, "This is really sad. I know how you must feel. How long ago was the divorce?"

"Sixteen years ago," Sandy answered.

Silence fell on the listeners. All thought the same thing — Sandy was wallowing in self-pity. This was a hang up for her. And everyone wanted to tell her, "Sandy, stop your pity party. Start building a life to run to, instead of running to a dead marriage for sixteen years."

Blaming

Blaming is an emotional hang up that gets nowhere. The cycle of "He did . . . ," no "She did . . . ," no "He did . . ." is placing responsibility for problems on someone else's shoulders. Blaming others is believing that you are helpless in solving your own problems of loss or pain.

Craig bitterly blamed his wife for his unhappiness. "She loved her sisters more than me. Every time I left town, off she would go. They would get together and go shopping, or get together and sew. She knew I didn't like them, but she thought they were fine people. Her sisters ruined our marriage. They knew they weren't welcome at my house and didn't come around anymore when I was there, thank goodness. If my wife had agreed that those sisters weren't worth the powder it would take to blow them all away, we would still be married."

Blaming is also shifting responsibility. If you can believe your ex is a jerk, that makes you the good guy, the wearer of the white hat. To continually make such statements as "She/he made life miserable" feeds your anger.

To get out of this trap and fix your flat, focus on your choices. You chose your former spouse; you chose your way of dealing with the situation; you made decisions along the way. You are to some degree responsible.

Living through Others

Living through others is a flat tire that stalls progress, too. It's usually a treatment for guilt, but only a sugar pill, not a cure.

Ethyl was speaking for other mothers when she said, "I felt like such a failure when I divorced that I overcompensated by being Super Mom. I also felt so guilty for going off to work each day that I thought I had to make up for lost time. So I spent my evenings and every weekend doing educational or recreational projects with the kids. I would do housework only after they were in bed so that I would not deprive them of our limited together time. I'm tired. I'm really tired. I've been living like this for five years. The worst part of our situation is that I'm beginning to resent the kids, and they have done nothing. I have done it to myself.

"I need to make a change. I need some adult conversation. I don't get it at work because I work a station completely by myself. I was sitting at the bus stop the other day when it started to rain. I turned to the lady next to me and said, 'Well, hear the pitter-patter of the rain.' She looked at me and didn't say anything. I felt like such a fool. I could not wait to get out of there. Don't you agree I need to make a change?"

Living through others can be a cruel hang up. Bitterness can set in when children leave, which they will do.

This living through others is an attempt to fill the emptiness, as well as erase the guilt. It is far better to build more relationships on your own and thus take care of yourself in order to keep on caring for others.

Flight from Self

Flight from self is indicative of your inability to face yourself. Even Ethyl's self-sacrifice to children could be an inability to face herself. If you keep your focus on your children to avoid facing yourself, you prevent your own recovery.

The flight from self becomes a hang up when you're running from yourself. Trying to run from yourself by drinking, by watching TV, by sleeping, hypnotism, workaholism or overscheduling, delays facing the reality of divorce and recovery. You cannot leave your problems by running from them. The problems seem to follow you right down the road. Then you risk starting over with the same problems. Don't run *from* something — run *to* something.

"I am so busy," Caty said. "I go to aerobics Tuesday and Thursday afternoons. I am a Brownie leader on

Mondays. I go to church Sundays and Wednesdays. I play bridge every other Tuesday night. I take golf lessons on Friday mornings. I have grandmother over every Thursday for quilting and lunch. I do hospital volunteer work Monday mornings. I don't have time to think anymore."

Too bad, too sad. She doesn't want to think any-more, but she needs to. She cannot run from herself in-definitely. Sure, she needs to seek the new life, but she also needs time to think and feel. She needs balance in her life.

Often divorcees live like a pendulum swing. One far swing is the frantic, busy life, trying to fill the empti-ness. Then a far swing to the other side — a stupor, lan-guid, limbo, lifeless existence. Finally, the pendulum settles somewhere in the middle as they get away from these emotional hang ups and repair the flats.

Cries of a Half-Person

This frantic running from self to avoid emptiness sometimes results in a frantic search for your other half. Those who fall into this trap have a quality of despera-tion about them.

Believing that being single is miserable and empty makes you feel miserable and empty. This feeling of emptiness can prompt you to fall strongly for the first person that exhibits some kindness toward you. This is an attempt to feel whole again.

To get away from this hang-up, build up your own life. Fill your life's bucket with worthwhile living. Sure, take a class, learn to cook, clean and care for yourself. Do whatever it takes to keep you alive, moving and in touch with the present, with reality and with yourself.

The cry that "I am only a half-person unless I am married," will not make a marriage based on love but a marriage coming from weakness. This cry is a trap. To get out of this trap, develop the attitude, "I am okay if single, okay if married."

It also helps to realize that the grass is not always greener elsewhere — grass everywhere still has to be fertilized, watered and mowed.

Philippians 4:11 says, ". . . for I have learned to be content whatever the circumstances." A positive attitude along this line is to say, "The best place to be is where I am."

Divorce Recovery Journal

As you begin your next entry in your divorce recovery journal, think about these emotional hang-ups, the flat tires that inconvenience your journey.

First, write a paragraph or more on the emotional hang-up that best describes where you are now.

Then finish this statement: The flat tire that keeps me from moving on is . . . Don't just complete the sentence, but write everything you think about your flat tire — how you got it, how long you have had it, what you did about it in the past and how you can fix it now. You must fix your flats in order to get on down the road again feeling good about yourself and to get on with building your self-esteem.

4

Rewind, Fast Forward or Eject

*L*ou began her story with a disclaimer one evening in divorce recovery class: "I know you'll all probably think I'm making up this story. It sounds like a poorly written script for 'As the World Turns' or something. But I'm sorry to say that it's true. Every lousy bit of it's true. I wish it weren't." Then she took a deep breath, sighed heavily and said, "Well, here goes.

"My husband was living a double life. He had two distinct life styles going at the same time. His life with me was family life. We had a home, children and yard work on Saturdays. We had the typical American dream — a three-bedroom brick house in the suburbs, a Chevrolet station wagon, two kids, two dogs and apple pie on Sunday. I was a housewife and mother. I thought marriage was a bed of roses.

"He is a manufacturer's representative. It's a good job, and Hal is good at his job. His job required that he go out of town about three times a month for just two or three days each time. Often these out of town trips were just for overnight. That wasn't so bad. Some of my friends' husbands were gone Monday through Thursday, so I thought this was a good arrangement. Hal did too.

"Then I found out why he liked this arrangement. This was his set-up for his other life. When he was *out* of town, he was actually *across* town, in another suburb on the other side of the metroplex. He had a different life going there.

"Actually there were similarities in the two lives. The home away from home also was a three-bedroom brick house in the suburbs with a Chevrolet station wagon, two kids and two dogs, but no apple pie on Sunday. Sundays Hal was always at our home. The difference is the woman. She isn't a housewife. She is a career woman, and she is 'adventuresome.' The houses were similar, but the lifestyles were drastically different.

FUN AND FREEDOM?

"Hal told me after the discovery that the biggest difference in the two lifestyles was the degree of fun. In his other home the atmosphere was carefree, amusing, laughing and no responsibility. His bubble burst when his career woman decided she wanted my lifestyle, to be a stay-at-home mother.

"Hal couldn't financially maintain two homes by himself. When he began to take a closer look at his life, he began to feel guilty and worried, and his distress was evident to me. I was sensitive to his distress. I didn't understand what was bothering him, but I knew something was. He wasn't himself around the house. Usually good-natured, he turned into a bear, a growling bear. I was very concerned about him.

"One Tuesday, while he was out of town, I decided to call him long distance to cheer him up. I didn't know where he stayed, so I called his secretary. She stuttered and stammered. She did not know what to say. Finally, she blurted, 'I don't know what to say. Hal doesn't go out of town. He is here every day.'

"I was stunned. I weakly mumbled something about my confusion and asked her to have him call me. She said she would.

"That evening Hal came home, and my life crumbled. I didn't want to hear what he would tell me, and he didn't want to tell it, but I could not shut up. I kept after him. I kept asking questions, knowing I did not want to hear the answers. I kept asking for details I did not want to know, but I asked anyway. I thought I had to know.

"We separated and filed for divorce. During the separation I continued to stay at home, but I thought I was going crazy. Staying at home no longer was a bed of roses. All I could think of was the lies and the horrible deceit. I have never felt like such a fool. I would think about the times he would come home when I would be sympathetic to his tiredness. Now I would get mad at myself for thinking he was tired from fun and adventure, not from hard work. I would think about the dull evenings we spent together. I had been content with quietness; he had been bored. So many memories kept going through my mind, I would actually get dizzy. I would even get sick.

"I had seen my life one way, but in reality it was something else. Now the memories are confusing. I keep going back over every holiday, every weekend, every night out, trying to determine what was fantasy, what was reality. The memories haunt me because now I don't understand. I didn't understand then either, but I thought I did.

"For months I was tormented by memories. I kept going back and going back in my mind. I wanted to figure out what had been going on. Where had the dream broken? The more I thought about it, the madder I would be, and the madder I would get, the more I was determined to figure out what was happening. I lived a vicious cycle in my mind.

"My sanity has begun to return. I am busy doing some necessary adjusting to my new lifestyle. Now I am working. Maybe I am an adventuresome career woman.

"I function normally most of the time, at least at work I do. I find it difficult to not think of myself as Hal's wife. Many months have passed, and when I go home from work it's different. When I'm home I think of the things I should do as a housewife — clean out closets, make grocery lists, plan meals. When I'm at work, I don't feel like a housewife.

"I am managing my life fairly well. I can sleep at night with the light out now, and I go to work in the daytime. I don't cry so much anymore. I feel like I'm adjusting to singleness, except for the memories."

In the weeks that followed, Lou continued to talk about her ambivalence and her transition from married to single adult. The transition is a slow process, and the memories are a stumbling block in this process.

THE PROPER PERSPECTIVE

Lou was really struggling to put her marriage in a proper perspective. She couldn't decide if her marriage had been wonderful or if it had been awful. She thought she was driving forward, but her eyes were constantly on the rearview mirror. Instead of driving, she was being driven to put a correct perspective on her marriage.

For Lou, marriage shaped her identity. Hers was the fairy-tale dream, contented life in the suburbs as Hal's uncomplaining wife. Marriage met her emotional needs for a long time. That was in the past now, but she could not come to terms with her past.

Too often people sacrifice their present to the god of the past by not putting the past to rest. This reluctance to break away from the past comes from a need to punish.

WHO FAILED?

"In trying to figure out what went wrong, I get torn up over who failed? For a long time I thought it was obvious that he did. 'Of course. That's it. He did me wrong.' But then I begin to think, 'I did him wrong too.' I get very confused."

Down deep Lou knew she had failed Hal, and she knew he had failed her. She was torn between wanting to punish him and wanting to punish herself. Because of her cyclic feelings, she was temporarily helpless and disoriented.

Renee told Lou, "I am troubled like you, Lou. Talk about being disoriented. That's me. I don't know who to kick the hardest either — me or Wilson.

"I wanted the divorce; he didn't. Because I'm the one who left, everybody is mad at me. The kids begged me to go back, to not hurt Daddy. I would feel so guilty, and I'd kick myself.

"Then I remember how bad it was. Nobody who is mad at me understands what I went through before making this decision. I didn't suddenly make a decision. I agonized over it. It was the hardest thing to do that I've ever done. But I had to do it. I couldn't take the abuse anymore. So I kick him.

"People who paint me as the bad guy don't know. We publicly presented ourselves as an all right couple. They think I wanted to punish him for something insignificant. Not so. They kick me.

"I went through the shock and anger stages while I was married. I didn't want my marriage to fail. I was very committed to Wilson and the making of a marriage. Maybe that divorce was my way of punishing him. I don't know. But divorce has punished both of us. I punish me for wanting the divorce. I punish him for pushing me into it. I kick us both, for different reasons.

"I keep trying to understand what I could have done differently. I know I brought on the divorce, but I don't want all the blame for it. I don't deserve it. I'm getting tired of defending myself, and I'm tired of blaming myself. I'm also getting tired of blaming him. I'm just tired, worn out. I'm tired of all this kicking around."

NEW GRIP ON LIFE

To begin driving forward, Lou and Renee needed a new grip on life. Their pasts were controlling them.

Yet, for all Lou's concentration on the past, she was realizing she could not fix it. The past was as it was. Today she couldn't rearrange it or manipulate it to make it fit her fairy-tale dream. She had no control over it. But, she wanted to get control of it. She wanted some control somewhere.

Forgiveness

The first step through the door from your past into your present is self-forgiveness. When you recognize that the past is just that — past, and that during that past period of time you made some mistakes, mistakes you cannot now correct, the only thing left is to forgive yourself and get on with living. You can't go back and relive those troublesome days. You can't fix what happened. It happened, and it's over. Life goes on, and so must you.

Often you are the last to forgive yourself and move on. Your friends have forgiven you, your family has probably forgiven you, and God has most certainly forgiven you. Now, it's your turn. Go ahead. Walk over to the mirror, look yourself straight in the eye, and say, "I forgive you." Now, say it again with more conviction, and try smiling this time as you say confidently, "I forgive you."

Once you have begun to forgive yourself, you can begin to forgive others, too, like your ex. When you realize you were not totally to blame for what happened, you may also be able to realize it was probably not totally your ex's fault either. You may be able to see your ex in a more realistic light — as a human being that makes mistakes, just like you. You may be able to *begin* forgiving the hurts and frustrations your ex caused. Only when that forgiveness occurs can you truly move into the next, more productive, stage of your life.

Forgiveness is the process of letting go of the past to live fully in the present and look forward to the future. Think about it.

Fill Your Bucket

One way of gaining control is to spend less time complaining about yesterday's problems and spend more time solving today's problems. It is easier to gain control and to let go of the past if your present day's life bucket is full.

Picture your life as the bucket you carry with you at all times. You get to decide what goes into your bucket. What you put into your bucket changes from time to time. If at the beach, you may choose to put water in your bucket. If in the mountains, you may collect rocks for your bucket. Sometimes you pick flowers for your bucket. Sometimes your bucket is half full, sometimes it is running over.

Your bucket is full if you have good things going for you — good friends, a good job and a good support system. The solving of today's problems involves taking steps to fill up your bucket with good things.

Acceptance

Another way of gaining control is to accept the divorce as the end to a destructive relationship, not as punishment for your failure. It has happened. Done, finished. Since it's impossible to go back in time to fix it, the present problem is in the heart. It won't go away. You must accept the reality — you are, or soon will be, divorced. And you *will* recover.

Find What's Right

Lou kept trying to find out what was wrong. She never looked for what was right. To add balance to her thinking, during the following weeks she began to focus on what was right about her, about Hal, and about her marriage. She began to accept her past as she did this.

Take an honest and positive glance at your marriage. Weren't there some good times? Didn't your ex do some really good things from time to time? Don't you have beautiful children that your ex and you gave birth to together? Don't you have some pleasant memories to cherish?

Challenge: Make a list of the positive things you can remember about your marriage. Let your mind wander through the pleasant memories and stop to smell the occasional, delightful fragrance of flowers that never fade. Look for what was right.

Changing Attitude

The heart can be changed. A change in attitude is necessary in coming to terms with the past, the memories of the past. Believe in change. Decide on change. This is what it takes.

While in the process of writing this chapter, I was visiting with Joyce Guest, a vibrant, bubbly, single friend of mine. To get a fresh opinion, I asked her, "Joyce, define memory for me."

She paused a moment, then replied, "I think memory is retrievable information that has made an impression sufficient enough to be recorded, as on a cassette tape."

I thought about this a minute. If memory is on a tape, I am the one who controls the recorder. I put in the tapes. I plug in the recorder. I can rewind, fast forward or eject the tape. The tape is nothing unless I do something with it.

In order to change an attitude, change the tapes. You can fast forward what you don't want to hear. You can even erase some bad tapes. You can record over it with new information. Memory is not set in concrete. It is recorded on tapes. Quit playing old tapes, and make new ones.

Remove Reminders

To get the tapes changed, it may be necessary to remove reminders. Juan had a strong opinion about removing reminders.

"When my wife left suddenly, I was so shocked that I didn't pay attention to my surroundings. Her closet was still full. Her make-up jars were on the bathroom vanity. I was accustomed to seeing them there, so I didn't really notice. After many months I finally gathered all her things, put them in bags and took them to a neighbor. I asked her to do with them as she pleased.

"I began to notice a big difference in myself after this walk to the neighbor's house. I began to relax more, and I began to feel more at home. I began to create some new dreams. I even began to plan a vacation to the mountains, something I had always wanted to do, but hadn't since Beverly never did like the mountains. Removing the reminders helped me become less emotional about the memories and to get on with living."

Learn from the Past

Memories are a part of life. Memories from childhood. Memories from high school. Memories from early marriage. Memories from late marriage. The events that make the memories *cannot* be changed. The attitude toward the memories can be changed.

In learning from the past, recognize weaknesses in order to build strengths. Lou began to recognize a weakness in her inability to have fun, to be carefree and to find humor. She is working on building a strength by recognizing and admitting the weakness.

As the attitude toward the memories changes, the emotional impact of the events changes. This is so necessary for getting on to the joyful life that awaits just by driving forward and filling our buckets with good things.

Socrates said, "The unexamined life is not worth living." Examine your memories, your yesterdays and learn from them.

Divorce Recovery Journal

To begin learning more from the past and coming to terms with it, get your divorce recovery journal out. Writing on these topics helps get a handle on memories. Moving on from the past to an adjusted present is an exciting move.

Write a paragraph beginning with each of these statements. Let the words flow so that you can move on with growth and change.

1. Part of the past that keeps haunting me is . . .

2. A damaging attitude I now have is . . .

3. What I can do about this attitude is . . .

4. What I have learned from the past is . . .

5

Flashbacks

"Flashbacks have had a disturbing effect on my life," Don told all of us. "I didn't know at the time that the experience I was having had a name. It was much later that I was told I was suffering from flashbacks.

"I had become very withdrawn and depressed. At first I wouldn't talk at home, to my wife or children. Then I wouldn't mix with others at work. Finally, I started missing work and just sitting at home. My wife had tried to talk to me when I started acting withdrawn, but she really became worried when I sat and stared and stayed home from work to just sit and stare.

TAKING CHARGE

"She built up her courage to take charge and took me to a psychologist. After only two sessions we knew that the problem was due to flashbacks from my war experience.

"In the army my buddy and I had paired off for a reconnaissance mission. We were out to find snipers. Our instructions were: If you hear a noise, shout out in Vietnamese, 'Show yourself,' count to two, then shoot."

Don looked serious as he continued. "We were trudging along doing our duty, at a leisurely pace. The jungle is really a very quiet place. Suddenly I heard a noise, and we stopped instantly. I called out, 'Show yourself.' No response. I shot the brush where the noise was. My heart was racing as I ran over to see what I had blasted, because I didn't just fire a single shot. I was so scared I shot as much as I could to be sure I was safe.

When I looked at my target, there was a woman and child. They looked to be Filipino. And I had blasted them. It was a horrible sight. I went into an uncontrollable rage right then. I screamed and yelled and stomped around, calling myself names. I was furious.

"My buddy and I buried the bodies and made our way back. I was then transferred to a hospital for two weeks. After the two weeks I felt fine. I had talked to nurses and doctors and other soldiers. Everybody understood how I felt, and I calmed down and really did feel okay. Tranquilizers helped too.

"I left the hospital and went back to finish my tour of duty. Then I went home, went to work and lived normally. I really was fine.

RECURRING VISIONS

"It was six years later that I became depressed and withdrawn. I'm really grateful that my wife took me to a good therapist. I sure didn't want to stay so withdrawn, but I couldn't seem to control the blahs.

"On my second session I began to open up and talk about the war experience. We had decided on my first visit that my depression had started when I was promoted and moved to a different office, yet I was excited about the promotion and transfer and really liked the people I worked with. But when I began to talk about the war, I had a sudden 'Aha! Click!'

"At the office a lady keypunch operator had an adopted Filipino child and a picture of the child sat on her desk, which I walked by many times a day. When this thought hit me, the tears began to flow as I relived my horror story.

"After I calmed down and got quiet again, the counselor simply asked me, "If you had known who was hidden in the brush, would you have fired?"

" 'Of course not! I wouldn't have shot a woman and child. I certainly wouldn't,' I said.

"She told me, 'Your motive was not to kill those people, so you don't need to keep punishing yourself for an accident. You had resolved this in the hospital to your satisfaction. But when you began to see the child's picture, you had flashbacks to that sad experience.'

"I lost 100 pounds of burden when she told me that. The simple words, 'If I had known . . .' were the keys to my soul. What a relief to be rid of the effects of flashbacks."

VETERANS OF DIVORCE

People in the divorcing process are veterans to the flashback phenomena. Flashbacks are memories from the subconscious, and in highly emotional states these convulsive memories emerge.

Going through divorce is an emotional state. Some may say it's an altered state of consciousness. In this alteration of life, many purposely play memory flashback and spend many hours thinking, "What did I do wrong? Where did this begin?"

Kristin said, "Many, many nights and days looking back consumed my every thought. I've kicked myself for gaining weight and asked if that was the problem. Once I was cooking lasagna and remembered the times when we were together that I fixed sandwiches for supper. Nobody complained. So I did it again and again, and now I wish I hadn't. I would repeat fusses in my mind, looking for the clue to this mess.

"Last Christmas I was shopping and something reminded me of an argument we had had while shopping for his brother one Christmas. Oh, I know something about flashbacks."

PROGRAMMED RESPONSES

"So do I," Judy said. "Last month my friend Justin asked if we could go out on a Saturday afternoon and cut wood for our fireplaces. In my divorce settlement I got custody of part of the tools, including a chain saw. So we took my chain saw to cut the wood.

"I had it serviced that morning with eager anticipation. I was enjoying the outdoors and being active. Then the chain saw started cutting out. It would die and Justin was working hard to keep it running. I became really anxious and started apologizing and explaining what I had done to prevent any foul up.

"Justin told me I was apologizing too much. Then he would tell me to quit being so defensive. Finally, he told me I was making him nervous and the saw wasn't, so I should shut up, and he kept trying to get the saw to run.

"After what seemed like a long time standing on one foot and then the other, pacing around trying to do something and apologizing, I said I wanted to go home.

"Justin asked, 'What is the matter with you?'

"I gave the typical female answer: 'Nothing.'

" 'There is something the matter. What is it?' He probed.

" 'Oh, nothing. I just want to go home,' I answered.

"So I took my chain saw and went home. I felt awful. I knew I was being ridiculous to get so upset over that malfunctioning chain saw and that I had looked foolish, and I couldn't understand why.

"Justin had been calm and patient with the saw and with me, yet I acted like I wanted to fight about it. My reaction really puzzled me.

"It was days later before I realized that I had gone through a flashback experience. When I was married, I was responsible for keeping everything in working order, that is, tuned up, filled up, sharpened, oiled, whatever it took so that when he wanted to use it, it was ready. If it wasn't ready, I had goofed. I was to blame, and it was a serious offense.

"Consequently, I was expecting Justin to chew me out for not having the chain saw running properly. I was programmed to be ready to fight. I was apologizing to avert the fight, to keep peace, but he wasn't playing the role I expected, that is, starting a fuss. I didn't know what to do. I just went home in a foul mood, mad at myself for fouling up. When I understood later what was happening, I quit being so mad at myself.

"But I do realize from this chain saw episode that flashbacks can seriously cut into my other relationships. Justin and I are still friends, but somebody else might not have been so understanding. Somebody else would have dismissed me as a kook."

Judy is right to realize flashbacks can interfere with other relationships and can cause us to make responses that don't fit the occasion. Merely knowing this helps you deal with it.

THEN AND NOW

Knowing that flashbacks will occur can help you recognize when it is happening. When you are making a response out of proportion or out of place, or unfitting to the situation, you can stop and remind yourself, "This is the wrong response. This is an old response to that previous situation and not at all necessary in this present situation."

Assess the present. Then give a true evaluation to the present situation. Judy might have had a better conclusion to her Saturday afternoon in the woods if she had stopped to think, "Justin is not the same person. He may not be the kind to attack me if the chain saw doesn't work. Why don't I look at the present situation and the present person before I react unreasonably?''

The Flashback Cork

Running from flashbacks doesn't solve the problem. That's like holding a fishing cork under water. When you relax your hold, it bobs back up. Running from the anxiety of a flashback forces it back into your subconscious. Eventually, it will resurface. Instead, deal with it. Stop and take a long, hard look at it. Stick with it a few minutes to understand what is really happening. Settle it in your mind so it doesn't bob back up later.

Response Admission

Then you can say, "I'm having a reaction that has nothing to do with you. I'm reacting to an old situation with a nonsense response because it doesn't fit here. Give me a minute, and it will pass." Such an admission will take you a long way toward getting control of the situation again.

Esther said, "When I was married my husband would say, 'Are you tired?' as his signal that it was time to leave, or he didn't want to make love, or even for me to be quiet. It was a game with us.

"I would respond, 'Yes, I'm tired,' as I was expected to, even though I wasn't. So I would prepare to leave, or turn over and go to sleep, or quit talking. But I didn't like the game, and I resented it. I felt manipulated.

"The first time my friend Josh asked me, 'Are you tired?' I snapped at him.

" 'No, I'm not tired. Quit asking me if I'm tired. I'll let you know if I'm ready to leave by saying, "I'm ready to leave." I'm not going to be trapped into that game.'

"He was stunned, and I was too. He couldn't believe I would lash out like that. I couldn't believe it either. I immediately started backstepping.

" 'I don't know why I said that. It doesn't make sense, does it? I know you aren't playing some vague game, and you aren't in the habit of asking, 'Are you tired?' I've really overreacted, and I don't know why.'

"My admission right then helped the situation. Over time I made the connection. I was emotionally responding to a past person and past situation. When I admitted this to myself and to Josh, we began to laugh at the phrase 'Are you tired?' It is funny now to think of how ridiculous I was in my intense flashback reaction to something so simple.

Choose a Proper Response

"Now I can simply say, 'No, I'm not tired,' or 'Yes, I'm tired.' Occasionally I feel a flash of anger at this question, but I can control it and choose a response appropriate to the situation and to the person."

Choosing a proper response is our way of dealing with the flashback constructively. Then with passage of time, those memories lose their intensity. Like Esther, with time we can even see how ridiculous the flashback reaction really is.

Abby laughed. "One of my flashback experiences has become humorous now. The memory is not painful or intense to me anymore, and I can enjoy telling it. But the first time after my divorce that a man asked me to go out on a boat, I said, 'Of course not. I don't ever want to go out on a boat. How dare you make such a suggestion. I'd rather remain friends than go boating. Don't ask me to set myself up for such a bad time.'

"The words just spilled out, and my tone of voice was harsh. I was adamant — I did not want anything to do with a boat. But I knew why.

"After we had been married about ten years, my husband decided we would get a boat and take up skiing and fishing. Sounded like a good idea at the time. The first time we went out was to Lake Grapevine for a trial run. About a half hour before dark, we headed back to the marina and he asked me, 'Do you want to get the truck and trailer down the ramp, or do you want to drive the boat up on the trailer?' I said I didn't know how to back up a trailer, and I'd rather drive the boat up.

"He went after the truck while I idled the boat in the harbor. When he got the trailer positioned on the ramp, I steered the boat in position, lined it up squarely, gave it the gas and headed for the V at the front of the trailer. Mind you, the only boat driving I had done was to pull a skier, and that's how I took off for that trailer. R-r-r-rmp! I went right through that V and into the bed of the truck.

"Now, a marina is always very noisy. Lots of people yelling, laughing, revving engines, kids screaming, even dogs barking. But when I drove the boat into the truck, an immediate hush fell on the place. It reminded me of that E. F. Hutton commercial that says, 'When E. F. Hutton speaks . . .' DEAD silence.

"We repaired the boat and the truck and made another run at fun on the lake. We went to Lake Texoma next. When it was time to leave, my husband said, 'This time I'll drive the boat. You bring the truck around. It is a four lane ramp and nobody is there. Just back straight down the ramp.'

"So I took the truck and started to back down this four-lane ramp. I would go back five feet, then the trailer would go to the left. I pulled up, backed down five feet and the trailer went to the right. For 45 minutes I went up, back, right, up, back, left, while my husband stood in the boat groaning and turning red — not from the sun either.

"Finally, some man came walking by. He asked if I needed help. I got out of the truck and said, 'Please back this truck down that ramp.' He did.

"We made the three-hour drive from Lake Texoma in silence, heavy silence. But we didn't give up. When we got home, the navigator told me I would learn how to back a trailer. The next day I was to practice in our driveway 'till I could do it. We had a circular driveway. I practiced entering from the left, and I practiced entering from the right. I practiced going down the straight of the driveway and around the circle. And I conquered. I did learn how to back that trailer, and was I proud. 'I'm ready now,' I thought.

"So off we go to Lake Livingston for another fun adventure. It came time to leave. No sweat. I knew what to do. I've practiced this. This ramp was only one lane. No problem. It was as wide as the driveway. I backed the truck and trailer down that ramp straight as an arrow. I grinned, feeling like a Cheshire cat, content and satisfied, 'till I heard him yell, 'Stop! STOP! STOP! Oh, no! Why didn't you stop?'

"Well, nobody had told me when to stop, and I was trying to get as close to the boat as I could. Now, I haven't tested all boat ramps, but that boat ramp had a big drop off at the end of the concrete. I had backed so far the trailer dropped off, still attached to the trailer hitch, but now hanging down in the water at a right angle to the truck.

"Pulling the truck forward wouldn't lift the trailer. That just made it bang against the ramp. And six men couldn't lift it up against the water. So, we had to call a maritime wrecker with a special winch that goes out into the water. After only a couple of hours we were out and on our way home — in silence, DEAD silence.

"As we approached home, I timidly asked, 'Do we want to continue having this much fun?' I really felt as if I'd had all the fun I could take.

"So when Leo asked me to go boating, I reacted. I suppose it was a flashback. I was responding in the present to a past experience. But I consciously knew why. Now I can respond with laughter, though, not with harshness."

That is what recovery to the flashback experience is all about. Realistically assessing the present situation, facing and admitting what is really going on, choosing a different, more appropriate response so that the emotional intensity is dissipated. Furthermore, resolving the experience with humor is good medicine, good therapy and good recovery.

Divorce Recovery Journal

Recall a flashback experience you have had. Write in your journal what a more appropriate response could be. Can you add humor to it?

6

The Dream Ends

And the handsome prince and the beautiful princess were married in a wonderful ceremony in the fairyland kingdom. And they lived happily ever after." That's the dream that we were bequeathed by our fairy-tale society. It was a glorious dream, and we cling to it with all our might.

The dreams are the last to go. We hold on to the dream of what should have been or what could have been. The dreams have been there for a long time. They are so hard to let go. When you can let the dreams go, you are moving ahead toward divorce recovery.

SEEKING FORGIVENESS

"Kennedy, this is your first time in divorce recovery class. Tell us something about yourself."

"My name is Kennedy. I am divorced. My divorce was final seven months ago. The marriage was over a long time before that, but I didn't know it. I love my wife and I want us to get back together, but every day that passes lets us become farther apart. The longer we are apart, the more independent she becomes. She has been by herself about a year now, and she is convinced she doesn't need me anymore.

"I'm not convinced I can live without her though. I've made serious mistakes. I'm what you call the 'guilty party.' I foolishly got caught up in passion and lost my head. I want to correct my mistakes. I can't though. I can't forgive myself for these mistakes.

"When the bad times started, my wife pleaded with me and I wouldn't listen. Men from church came to see me, as they should, and I thought they didn't understand and didn't know what they were talking about. They said I would regret this, and I do.

"Friends pleaded with me, but I wouldn't change. Then when I did come to my senses, it was too late.

"For months I begged for forgiveness. I've gone to the friends and asked for forgiveness. I've asked for forgiveness at church. I've certainly asked for God's forgiveness. I've asked for my wife's forgiveness. She can't provide it.

"I have been greatly tormented. My counselor told me to come here. He said I would get some of the acceptance I need here."

Wow! We thought we would get name, number of kids, how long divorced, where employed, but we got a lot more.

"Welcome to divorce recovery class. You certainly are accepted here. It sounds as if your biggest problem right now is a struggle with forgiveness."

"Sure is," Kennedy went on to say. "I know God forgives me. Some of you may think I don't deserve that, but I do, and my Bible tells me God forgives a repentant heart. I know my repentant heart, and I know God has forgiven me.

"The real problem is I can't forgive myself. I can't forgive myself because she won't forgive me. I feel so guilty, because I am. This hurts, knowing I've done wrong and can't correct it. But, I'm working on it. I know I have to wrestle with it myself. I don't intend to always feel as bad as I do right now."

To heal the festering pain, Kennedy needed the spiritual iodine of forgiveness. Without forgiveness the hurts fester into resentment. When you get a sticker that festers, you open it up for drainage and healing.

Open Up

The same is true for emotional hurt and guilt. You must open up for drainage. To do this you open up your mind and let the grievance flow out. You unburden yourself. God calls this confessing your sins.

Kennedy was certainly doing the right things for healing. He was confessing his sins. He was seeing a counselor and unburdening himself. He was in divorce recovery class letting the grievance flow out among friends.

"Kennedy, have you considered writing a letter to your ex-wife asking for forgiveness? You don't have to mail it if you don't want to, or you can if you want to. The important thing is that by writing a letter asking for forgiveness, you may get the relief you need."

"I've thought about it. In fact, I've started a letter. I just can't seem to get it finished," he said.

Study the Factors

A decision for writing a letter was not reached that evening, but further discussion helped. Kennedy and others in class made sincere efforts to study the personality factors which created unhealthy situations so that patterns would not be established and repeated. Kennedy was quite certain he had learned many lessons from his torment and wouldn't be repeating his mistake. He had already accepted his responsibility for his divorce.

In this discussion Danielle said, "I can accept the fact that I had a responsibility in the divorce, and I forgive myself, or I rationalize that I did the best I could with the information I had at the time. I don't struggle with myself, but I can't forgive my husband. I'm too mad to forgive him, and besides, he hasn't apologized. He couldn't care less whether I forgive him or not. Anyway, what he did to me was wrong, and you can't change that.''

Agreed. You can't change what has happened, but you can change how you feel about it. You can heal the hurt that comes from what has happened.

You can do this because forgiveness is a decision, not a feeling. It's a decision that changes your feelings. It's a decision to give up your right to hurt back.

Excuse for Hatred

Not to give up the right to hurt back is an excuse for hating. Hating destroys the hater, not the hatee.

Forgive then, for your sake, so you can be free of hate. A hating heart separates you from other people, and you need people.

PUTTING A HALT TO HATE

To stop hating another person, you forgive him by mentally accepting the person but not his act that hurt you. You don't tolerate what a person does when you forgive him for doing it. You forgive the person and refuse to tolerate *what* he has done. Separate the person from the hated action.

A Different Look

To separate out the person, practice looking at the person differently. For instance, see the person as insecure, needing love, struggling for happiness, feeling defensive or fallible. In this different light, you can begin to say, "I want my ex to find happiness." This is the beginning of forgiveness. And forgiveness is the beginning of divorce recovery.

Zap Experience

Forgiveness has a beginning and is a process. It's not a zap experience. Therefore, allow the needed time for your heart to change and heal. If your heart doesn't change, and you hold on to a painful past and hate, bitterness and resentment become your future.

Power to Forgive

To make your future better, choose to love, not to hate or to get even. Filling your heart with love gives you the power to forgive.

With love you wipe the hurt away, as a mother washes away the dirt from a child's face. With love God forgives. He changes his memory, and what you did becomes unimportant. What he feels about who you are is important. This is the process you go through in forgiving yourself and others.

Forgive and Forget?

Danielle came back with, "I can't forget the act. That's impossible. I might be able to separate the person from the act, but I can't forget the act; so the hurt goes on."

Forgiving is not forgetting. If you can forget, forgiving is not necessary. It is because of the memory that forgiving is needed. The purpose of forgiveness is to make the memory no longer painful and to heal the hate. Forgiveness is how you let go of the pain.

Empty Your Gunny Sack

If you have never picked cotton, visualize the scenes from *Gone with the Wind* showing the people picking cotton. They walked down long rows of cotton plants dragging a gunny sack, a burlap bag. They picked cotton and pitched it in the bag, took a step, picked and pitched it in the bag. They walked the length of the row picking the cotton and pitching. At the end of the row, they emptied their sack into a big cotton bin and started down the next row.

Saving up the hurts that come your way is like picking cotton. You get one and put it in your gunny sack. Then you get another and pitch it in. The bag gets full and heavy, but you keep dragging it. When you get to the end of the row, instead of emptying your gunny sack of all the hurts you had collected, you could drag it down the next row, but it sure would get heavy.

The plantation owner came up with a plan that would keep you from wearing yourself out. You can empty your gunny sack through forgiveness and have a new beginning on that next row. Then you don't get all bent out of shape carrying such a heavy load. You won't forget that first row. You experienced it. But you can get relief, and you get a fresh start by emptying your gunny sack.

Write the Letter

Kennedy came back the next week and said, "I emptied my gunny sack. Or at least I feel like I did. I finished the letter I had started. I'd like to read it to you and see what you think."

Dear Reba,
I know it's over. I suppose it ended a long time ago, but I'm just now realizing it. I apologize for the pain I caused you. I hope you are happy. I wish the best for both of us. I don't hold any grudge or ill feeling and hope you don't either. I still have fond memories of our past. Forgive me.

Kennedy

Everyone thought it was a fine letter and congratulated Kennedy.

Kennedy said, "I had to do this. In order to become the kind of person God wants me to be, I had to ask for forgiveness. And I've had to start the process of forgiving myself.

"When we talked about the gunny sack, I realized I couldn't have a new row being burdened with my full bag. I care that I did wrong, and I won't do it again. But I can't let this wrong curse me every day.

"I'm in the process of separating the 'who I am' from the 'what I did.' At first I couldn't, but now I tell myself, 'The act of a jerk yesterday doesn't make me an everlasting jerk for tomorrow.' I can be a useful Christian if I don't hang my head for the next 40 years."

What rejoicing! Kennedy was such a neat guy to risk his honesty with all of us. He was certainly vulnerable here, but we all learned from him. We learned what a struggle forgiveness is.

A NEW BEGINNING

Danielle admitted forgiving is a struggle. "I'm not ready yet. The wrong here is a reality. I can agree that I am holding on to pain and that I don't have a loving heart. I don't want to stay this way. I've never been a hating person, and I don't want to be, but forgiving my ex? Not yet."

Kennedy told her, "I can understand how you feel. It seems that you think if you forgive your former mate, you are accepting his behavior. Then you would get a bad deal, and he gets off the hook. But really, forgiving is the best deal. Without it, the malice will destroy you, and you're too valuable a person to let malice destroy you. Don't give up. You'll come up with a good deal for you. It's a slow process that takes a lot of effort. I know you'll make it."

She will make it. She will make it because she is committed to making a new beginning. Forgiveness is the beginning of the joyful, abundant life that awaits you. Forgiveness is what you go through in order to come to terms with the past, to let go of the hurts and injustices.

A forgiving heart heals negative emotions, the traps that keep you stuck on the wrong side, fixes the flat tires and empties the gunny sack. It enables you to develop friendships and healthy relationships, to heal and be happy, and repair the shattered dreams.

It enables you to get right in your relationship with God.

> *Dear Lord,*
> *Please help me*
> *To accept others as they are,*
> *To understand shortcomings and make allowance for them,*
> *To work patiently for improvement,*
> *To appreciate what people do right, not criticize what they do wrong,*
> *To be slow to anger, slow to speak, and quick to listen,*
> *To rise above the hard fall,*
> *To live with my broken dreams.*

Divorce Recovery Journal

Please continue to write in your divorce recovery journal until you can't think of anything else to say.

In particular at this time write what you think is the hardest part of forgiveness for you.

7

Plop, Plop, Fizz, Fizz

Postmortems don't last forever. In the divorcing process, you can't keep sitting at the postmortem. You have to get on with the funeral and the burial. Moving on to the postburial stage requires making changes. Changes in life can be difficult, even painful, but holding on to a painful past isn't any better. When the past is painful, there is nothing to lose (and everything to gain) in going through the difficulty of change in order to have a better future. The changes can only result in growth and a pain-free existence.

THE CHALLENGE OF CHANGE

In a small group discussion at an out-of-town seminar Chuck was eager to talk about the changes in his life during the last two years.

"When my wife said she wanted a divorce, I was furious, and I thought she was crazy. I had never done anything to her. I was an okay husband. I wasn't the perfect Tom Selleck or a soap opera romancer, but I was okay, like everybody else. If she wanted anything else, she must be off her gourd. I thought she was tearing up a home over nothing. It didn't make sense. How dare she find fault with me! No complaint could be so serious as to call for a divorce. I could not believe my ears. Nothing I said made any difference. Her mind was made up. She had always listened to me before, and I couldn't figure out anything to say that would make her listen again. I would talk softly — it didn't matter. Then I would yell — it still didn't matter. Nothing I said mattered any more. It was so frustrating. I just knew she had gone crazy. That was the only explanation. Everything was crazy to me now.

"Despite all my pleading, she went through with it. I quit my job. It wasn't going to last much longer anyway, and I just couldn't face the people at work every day. I didn't see any purpose in working anymore.

"I would sit in her driveway and wait for her to come home. She never was really ugly to me, just politely cool. For months I just drifted. Many nights I slept in the van, either in front of her house or parked down in the park. Occasionally I would work, a day here, a day there, once for a whole week picking up trash along the highway and putting it in plastic bags. All the time I was thinking, 'If only we could get back together,' or 'What if I worked regularly again,' or 'If only I had remembered her birthday,' or 'If only I hadn't gone to the drag races every Saturday.'

LEARNING TO LISTEN

"About five months after the divorce, one Friday when she came home from work I was sitting in her driveway having these thoughts and wanting to talk to her. When she drove up, she stopped and talked to me and even listened to me. I listened to what she said this time. She probably had said the same thing before, but this time I listened.

"She patiently told me, 'Chuck, you're going to have to change, not for my sake, but for your sake. Whether we get back together or not, you still have to change. You can't keep going through life not taking charge. You are the captain of your ship, but you don't act like it. Your ship drifts at sea as though without a captain. I don't want to talk to you anymore until I can see some change in you. You tell me you will change. For me to tell you what to do — that won't work. The change needs to come from within *you*, not from me.'

"She said more, and I listened. I thought about all she told me for many days to come. I did begin to change, and I am still changing. I have done a lot of soul-searching, and I am coming up with some answers, answers that give me some direction to my life, some direction to my ship.

ADMITTING THE TRUTH

"It has been slow, very slow and difficult. Nobody knows how difficult it has been, but I have changed. First, I had to admit that I truly did need to change. That wasn't the hardest part though. It was obvious even to me that I needed to change. The hardest part was that I had to admit to myself that I had not been okay as a husband. I had job-hopped continuously, and we had moved a lot. I always had a job, and I thought that was enough, but it wasn't. Now I have settled down to one job and work every day. Major change. As I got comfortable with this for a few months, I began to look at other changes I need to make.

"And then I began to admit I really had not taken any responsibility for the marriage. Jody had told me this for years, but I didn't pay any attention to what she was saying. Many hours of counseling taught me what this meant.

"When we were together, I had played a lot. I used to think because I didn't play around on *her* that it didn't matter how much I played around. Now I realize, it does matter. I have thought about this by the hour. After studying this I'm now much more aware of what it takes to be a good husband.

"I've read and I've talked. I read more books now in one year than I had read in 30 years. I talked to our minister and to other divorcees, which has really helped me see things differently.

NEW DIRECTION

"For the last 15 months my ship has taken a new direction. I am working full time at the same job I had last year. That's a major change for me. I'm going to school now, too. It took a lot of courage for me to make this change. Going back to school was really frightening. I didn't know how to register. I didn't know where the administration building or the classrooms were. And everybody on campus was young. But I went.

"I'm getting a degree in sociology. I would like to do something to help other people. I wish now I could tell everybody, 'Don't throw your life away like I have been doing. There's no reward in it.'

NEW HOPE

"Life isn't easy. Changing isn't easy. I still don't have many friends. I still love Jody, and I still want us to get back together, but at least now I know that the future is going to be better.

"Before I didn't care if I had friends or not. Now I care, and I'm doing things to make friends. I don't know why it scares me to meet people, but it always has. It's getting easier though.

"I used to never think about the future. It scared me to look ahead. But now I think about it. I used to think 'What difference does it make? What will be, will be.' Now I realize after all these months of thinking in loneliness that *I* make happen whatever happens. I am definitely changing. And the change is coming from within, like Jody said it should. I am still a young man, and there is time left to get my ship going in the right direction. Actually, it feels good to be more in control of my life, to know more about what is in store for me next week and even next year. I don't feel good yet, but I sure feel better.

"Jody and I are still good friends. I don't sleep in her driveway anymore, but I see her once in a while. She sees the change in me. She likes me better now, and I like me better. Her opinion is still important to me.

"Changing is so hard, but I highly recommend it. I'm not the same person I was three years ago when this mess started. I'm not as afraid of the future as I was. I have picked myself up by my bootstraps, and I'm a heavyweight."

MOTIVATED BY PAIN, PREVENTED BY FEAR

Chuck's experience with change is similar to the experiences of many divorcees — painful and slow.

In the beginning Chuck could not progress because his thinking was stuck on "If only . . ." and "What if . . ." Being stuck there prevented his growth. That way of thinking did not solve his problems. His pain motivated change, but his fear prevented change.

Fear of Flaws

Fear was behind Chuck's foolish pride. He was afraid to admit that he was less than a giant. He was afraid to admit he had failed. He was afraid to commit to the marriage and to his future.

As long as Chuck could say he was an okay husband and she was crazy, he was not admitting to being flawed. He was afraid to be honest with himself or about himself. You may think that admitting to being flawed invites rejection. And nobody invites rejection. So to avoid rejection, you hide your flaws, thinking no one can accept you with your imperfection.

Freedom of Flaws

The reverse is true. When you admit that you are less than perfect, people respond favorably to your honesty, knowing that they too are less than perfect. By your admission, you give others the freedom to be honest also. Then the burden of pretending to be a giant is lifted. When you hide yourself in the costume of a giant, you are restricted to that costume and are less free. You and those around you need the freedom to be honest and authentic in order to change and grow. The fear of rejection which prevents honesty also prevents the growth through change that is needed for divorce recovery.

QUICK FIXES

The change which results in growth in the divorce recovery process is truly taking lemons and making lemonade. Dr. Paul Faulkner, in his book *Making Things Right When Things Go Wrong* (Sweet, 1986), calls this "changing scars to stars."

Microwave Recovery

In order to make lemonade, in addition to admitting imperfection, you have to realize change takes time. There are no quick fixes, no microwave divorce recoveries, but progress is coming. Changing from the past to the future is taking two steps forward, one step back and sometimes dragging a foot.

Donald came to divorce recovery class his first time and announced, "I want the Plop, Plop, Fizz, Fizz Relief. I don't have a lifetime to devote to recovery."

He intended to be amusing, and he was, especially to those who had been in class six months or more who also had entered wanting immediate jet-age results.

Recovery from emotional pain takes time, but progress is being made when steps are being taken toward change.

A Bull by the Tail

Time alone will not make the necessary changes in life. Taking responsibility is also required. When Jody told Chuck he needed to be the captain of his ship, she was telling him to take responsibility for his life, to take charge.

Mark Twain said, "Anyone who has had a bull by the tail knows five or six things more than someone who hasn't." Well, Chuck took the bull by the tail when he began to face himself honestly. That was his first step.

The next step he took was to get help. He talked to his minister and other divorcees. Others have gone to classes and turned to friends. Chuck also read self-help books, just as you are doing now. See? Help is on the way.

Divorcees must also take responsibility for their own welfare. Chuck was taking responsibility for his welfare when he stayed with a job and went back to school. He knew he had to change. Where he was felt bad, and he was not going anywhere. He was proud of the new direction in his life, the new direction of his ship. He called it pulling himself up by his own bootstraps.

THE TURNING POINT

Taking responsibility for the change and growth one needs is the turning point to a new life. Committing to a new way of life requires taking courageous steps down the rocky path of change.

Turning to God

The first step is making a commitment to grow spiritually. To do this many divorcees turn to the church. Christians offer counseling and classes through the church to meet the emotional needs of people, especially at a time of crisis. Divorce is a crisis time, and a turning point in life, a change point.

At this turning point, many singles also turn to God in prayer, as well as to the church for consolation and answers. An increase in prayer life is definitely a spiritual growth step. It is spiritual growth, more than anything else, that helps a hurting person commit to a new life with God. About spiritual growth, I always say, "I can't get home without it."

During the divorce dilemma, stability and constancy are healers. The Bible says, "Jesus Christ is the same yesterday, today and forever" (Hebrews 13:8). Is it any wonder that he is also described as the Great Physician? And who else besides Jesus could understand the heart of a single person so well — he was tempted by the Devil alone in the wilderness, he stood alone against the "brood of vipers" of his day, he prayed alone in the garden while his friends slept, he even died alone on Calvary while his Father turned his face away from him.

Turning to God and his Son is the single smartest thing a single-again person can do to fully recover from the pain and desolation of divorce. By getting to know God better, you also get to know yourself better. It is through this mutual knowledge of self through God and his Word that life begins to turn around. You turn from shadows to sunshine and from vacuum to victory.

Turning to a New Identity

Committing to a new life is committing to a new identity. So often much of your identity was anchored in your marriage. Now you must return to your own identity as an individual.

Amy said, "I could sense a change in my identity when I changed my checking account after my divorce. I had always signed checks 'Mrs. David Murphy.' When this changed to 'Amy Murphy,' I liked the look of it. It was strange at first. I thought people might think I was forging checks, but nobody did.

"Then I began to take pride in the look and sound of Amy Murphy. I know this is a simple thing, but it was a big deal to me at that point. I felt like signing my name as Amy would make people notice that I was a person with a name of my very own."

Chuck was turning to a new identity as a student, as a long-term employee and as a responsible man. These were choices he made that gave him pride.

You can choose your new identity. You have to make changes anyway; so make the changes you have always wanted to make.

The third step in committing to a new life is to commit to a new personal life, which involves new friends, a new social structure and self-improvement projects.

Turning to New Friends

Just when you need friends the most, you look around and ask, "Where did they all go?" Your married friends don't know how to react to your new situation. They don't know what to say. They don't want to take sides. They don't want to get involved. And they certainly don't want your misfortune to rub off on them. So they don't call. They don't invite you over. They just don't do anything.

So, you make new friends — people who are positive minded and healthy spiritually. You find these people on common ground, at the places where you would have something in common, such as on the golf course, in the library, at a class on photography, at a church singles' class, at the women's center.

Karma told us that to meet new friends, she learned to play bridge. "I went to the junior college and took a course on beginning bridge. My parents had always played, and I knew it would be fun. I learned and learned well. This opened new doors for me. Now I go to the recreation center on Thursday nights and play. I even entered a tournament and had a great time. I have met a lot of people who invite me over, and I return the invitations. Learning bridge has been a blessing in my life."

Turning to Self-Improvement

You also meet new friends by getting involved in self-improvement projects. There are two benefits to this: the new people you meet and the self-improvement.

You may want to improve yourself by learning a new language. You take a class or join a conversation group. You can go to the Y for exercise classes, or take painting lessons, or go to the high school track and jog or walk. There are always other adults there, wherever you go, doing the same thing you're doing.

Turning to a New Social Structure

The new friends and the self-improvement projects develop into a new social structure that is of your own making, of your own decisions about commitment to a new life. Your new life required changes in your behavior and results in changes in you.

Turning to Help

The growth and changes in your life will inspire you to begin to give help to others. As your social structure changes, you begin to see others who need a friend. With others you begin to dream again. So, not only do you benefit from making new friends, those that you be-friend benefit also.

Shana told us one evening, "I saw a write-up in the paper about volunteers. It was a plea for people to take the training for counseling battered women. Ordinary people could do it. I decided this would be something to help me take my mind off myself, and I could volunteer for weekends, which are long for me anyway. I have discovered that giving this help has been great for me. I benefit the most, although I really do help others. I'm glad I do it."

DEVELOPING LOVE

The key to growth is developing love. Making new friends is developing love, and through a loving heart comes the desire to help others. This change is what inspired Chuck to major in sociology. He now wants to help others.

As I think about developing a new personal life and developing love, I think about my mother, Doris Massie. She lost both her husband and her health within a short span at a young age. For health reasons she moved a thousand miles away from home to Arizona.

She was forced to make new friends alone. She had to reach out. She soon made new friends in the church and elsewhere. Because walking was good for her lungs, when she was able to breathe again, she joined a hiking club. She made friends there, and it was a self-improvement project also. Her health and her long-distance move forced her to develop a new social structure.

In this new structure, she has grown full cycle, and she gives help to those who have lost health, lost spouses and lost lifetime homes. She is a delightful person with her new identity, but it was not easy. She was extremely lonely and sick when she first moved. She had to force herself to make the decision to change and improve her life.

The Independent Person

Before her loss of husband and health, Mom was a feisty, independent lady who gave the impression of saying, "I don't need your help. I'll take care of this." In her time of need, she moderated this statement to say, "Well, actually I do need you." Often the very independent person pushes people away, while yearning for closeness.

Sometimes people going through divorce overreact with independence and push people away, when it's people they need the most in order to recover. A crisis situation calls for people. As John Drakeford said, "It is by people we are broken, and it is by people we are put together again."

The Dependent Person

On the other hand, the very dependent person cries, "Someone take care of me," "I can't decide," "I *need* you," "Please take over." The dependent person pushes people away by begging for closeness — the opposite of his or her intent.

These two extremes of personality types often surface at the distressful times in life, whether it be over loss of health or loss of marriage.

The best balance is to be some of both with sincerity. You do need people, or at least *want* people. And you *can* take care of the situation but with help from others. This approach makes the see-saw balance better.

Glad to Be Alive

The loss of marriage is a major change in life. What you do with this change point is your decision. Your best decision is to make this change point a commitment to a new life that says, "I'm glad to be alive."

With a good balance between independent and dependent personality traits, honesty with self, help from others and a new sense of responsibility, that glad-to-be-alive feeling comes. That's how it worked with Chuck, that's how it worked with Mom. You get to make the decision for change and growth to work for you.

Divorce Recovery Journal

One way to help you make the changes is to continue with your divorce recovery journal. Writing helps you get a handle on the turmoil.

For this chapter's journal entry, think about and write on the following:

1. What change has been forced on you?

2. What change has been voluntary?

3. List at least ten ways you can add balance to your new life.

8

The House of Horrors

Have you ever walked into the house of horrors at a carnival? It's a room full of mirrors, each one different, reflecting a grotesque image of you and always changing. One time you see a tall, skinny you. The next time it's a short, fat you. Then you're fat at the top and skinny at the bottom.

It's a room of confusion. You stumble and grope your way through from one ugly reflection to the next, always wishing you could just find the exit and get out of there. There are some funny things about it, but for the most part it's an uncomfortable and unnerving experience.

This walk into the house of horrors is comparable to your relationship with your former spouse. The relationship changes as rapidly as walking from one mirror to the next in that room full of mirrors. And some of the views are just as grotesque and shattering.

Sometimes you can talk to your former spouse. On another occasion there is no talk, just quarreling. The atmosphere is unpredictable. A person you once viewed as precious becomes a raging, unreasonable maniac. It doesn't make sense. That person is always changing, and our feelings about that person are always changing. Sometimes these changes preceded the divorce; sometimes they follow. It makes you wonder, "What's up?"

THE TWO-FACED MIRROR

Floyd's relationship with his former spouse was always changing, and he could not get a handle on how to view her. Floyd was faithful in coming to divorce recovery class. He was so open with the group that all hearts were moved when he spoke. Over a period of months the change in him was truly dramatic. The change in his relationship with his ex-wife was equally as dramatic.

When he talked about his ex in the beginning, his voice spewed venom. "I hate her. I'll always hate her. She has turned my life upside down. She has caused me suffering that I never dreamed was possible. It has been a nightmare. I wouldn't make a dog go through what I have been through. Oh, how I hate her. I trusted her, and she has humiliated me."

The rest of the class listened. We knew. We understood the strong emotion. Everyone could identify with the rage he was feeling. Expressing his rage was helpful to him, and we wanted to be of help.

A couple of weeks later he came into class rather subdued. He sat quietly listening for about half an hour. Then something was said that triggered him.

"I had a long talk with my ex this weekend. I have tried many times to talk to her, and she would hang up on me or refuse in some way. I have written her letters, and she would not respond. My mind has been in such turmoil. I thought if we could talk, I would understand and feel better. If I could only get some whys answered, I thought, I could release that part of my life. Well, for the first time in eight months, we talked."

His voice was breaking as he continued with his story, "The talk was what I wanted. To be able to talk to her was so important to me that I had written down an agenda titled 'Future Conversation with Andrea,' and I kept this by the phone, just in case I ever got the opportunity to talk to her.

"Saturday morning I had to call her to make arrangements for visitation. I called so early that the kids were still asleep. She answered, and her mood was more receptive to conversation for a change. I begged her to not hang up but to talk awhile.

"I got some answers all right. She finally opened up and was honest with me in a kind way. She was not stinging and jabbing like before. I understand better now how this divorce came about. What I don't understand is how I could still love her? I hate her, and I love her. It doesn't make sense." For Floyd it was like looking into a two-faced mirror at the carnival.

At this point he was crying, and others cried with him. Everyone had understood when he said he hated her, and everyone understood when he said he both hated *and* loved her.

LOOKING FOR THE NATURAL MIRROR

Annilee responded to Floyd through her own quivering voice.

"I know how you feel. I've felt the same way. I've hated Rex, and I've loved him. I think though that I could describe it better by saying I feel strong emotions about Rex. After all, he sure was the center of my life for fourteen years. I had built all my dreams around him. We shared so much for so long — our home, our kids, our struggles of getting a business started. He was my best friend. I haven't just lost a husband; I've lost my very best friend."

"That's it," Floyd said. "I've lost my best friend. In fact, I think I've lost my only friend. I hate her for taking away my best friend, and I love her for having been my best friend.

"I'm torn up now because, in our Saturday morning conversation, she was a good friend again, even though we are divorced. Will I ever feel neutral? Or will I always love and hate?"

Others in class assured him that in time the tour through the house of horrors would be over, that he would find the exit and eventually escape to the real world. The time would come when she would no longer have that volatile, emotional impact.

"I'm looking forward to that. We have never had a knock-down-drag-out fight, but sometimes I want to knock her down and drag her out. Then I want to hug her and kiss her and cuddle her. I am tired. I want neutrality."

Jim Smoke in *Growing Through Divorce* describes the five emotional steps you go through toward neutrality with your former spouse. And they work.

Vindictive

In the beginning divorcees feel vindictive. The one wanting the divorce feels vindictive in getting the divorce. The divorce is a way of getting back at the spouse for past hurts. The one *not* wanting the divorce feels vindictive, too, and says, "I'll burn you back for this."

Hostility

Divorcees also feel hostility and so much anger. Both people are extremely angry. I don't believe anyone has gone through divorce without feeling a great deal of anger over it or the problems that lead to it.

Apathy

After a while though, the anger subsides. The brain takes over the body again, and you quit having the need to ram your fist into the wall. The next phase of feeling toward your ex is apathy. You get tired of worrying about it; you just don't really care anymore. The ex is no longer worth so much trauma.

Relief

After feeling apathy, you begin to feel relief. Jolene expressed this well when she said, "I'm relieved to be out of that mess. I didn't want the divorce. I wasn't ready to give up on the marriage, but now that it's over and I'm over the shock and all those other things we go through, I'm relieved. It was so hard to try to keep peace; it was very hard. I walked on egg shells for ten years. Now I'm relieved to not have to put up with what I was putting up with.''

Okay

Feeling okay about your ex is the final stage of the changes you go through. The time finally comes when life is okay in general, then you feel okay toward the ex, too. You don't love, and you don't hate. It's just okay. This is the mirror of neutrality Floyd looked for.

SHOCK WAVE

Even if you're in the stage of relief or okay toward your former spouse, there may still be some shocks coming your way from that person. Just knowing ahead of time what to expect may take some of the electricity out of the shock.

Surprise

One of the shocks you can anticipate is when you run into your former spouse unexpectedly.

''My ex and I had always used the same family doctor. I was so shocked when I ran into him in the waiting room at the doctor's office. I hadn't seen him in a long time. It was really awkward. I didn't know what to say, and yet I felt as if I ought to say something. I didn't want not to speak. But I didn't want to greet him with a peck on the cheek like we had always done. So I said, 'Hello, how are you?' and he grumbled something. I should have said, 'Oh, I see you still grumble in the mornings. Too bad.' But I didn't. We didn't talk. I was glad to get out of there. It was awkward.''

Tammy isn't the only one who can tell of an unexpected meeting. You can prepare yourself for it by knowing it's coming, perhaps not at a set time and place, but it *is* coming sometime. Knowing it's probable and anticipating it may keep you from being disturbed by it when it happens.

New Friend

You should also realize in advance that the day may come when you will see your former spouse with a new companion. This may have happened for some of you before the divorce. If it hasn't happened yet, you should expect it.

When we discussed this in class, Carl told us that he frequently sees his ex with her new boyfriend at his son's Little League games.

"At first it was very strained for me, and I couldn't keep my eyes off them. Of course, I didn't want them to see that I was watching; so, I tried to look nonchalant. I looked as nonchalant as a gnat swallowing an elephant. After a time or two, I could watch the game and not watch them all the time. I was so curious to see if she was different with him. She was. That really bothered me, but not enough to keep me away from my son's games. So, I said to myself, 'Carl, buck up. You've gotta do what you've gotta do. Make it good.' It's fine now."

Vicki couldn't say the same thing. She told us the girlfriend of her ex bought a house in the next block so that Kenny could be with *her* and near *our* kids.

"I can't stand it. I drive by there often, not to spy, but because I have to go that way. That's the direction to the kids' school.

"I'm going to sell my house and move the kids and me across town. I think asking me to tolerate being only a block away from them is asking too much. I can't do it."

Her reaction is understandable and common. This turn of events was too sudden for her. She did not have time to prepare for the shock.

Seeing your ex with a new companion is a shocker. As the Boy Scouts say, "Be prepared!"

New Mate

The final shocker in seeing your former spouse again happens when you meet the new mate. It probably will happen. Probably it will happen in a civilized setting too, like a graduation, wedding or funeral. In this setting everyone is expected to act civilized. How are you going to act? What are you going to say?

To be prepared for these upcoming events, know they are imminent. You can also know that, as you fill your life's bucket, these situations are not such shockers. You cannot control all of life's events, but you can control your reaction to these events. As you regain mastery of your switchboard, no one else can punch your buttons. So, don't turn control of your switchboard over to an ex, or an ex's new companion or new mate. As you regain mastery of your life, the emotional impact of these events fades away.

A NEW LOOK AT YOUR OLD RELATIONSHIP

Here are some guidelines for regaining mastery of your life and for taking a new look at your old relationship. These guidelines will help prepare you for the surprises that may arise. They certainly will help you be the one in the driver's seat.

Clean Break

First of all, when it's over, it's over. When it's over, make the break. Make a clean break. When the war is lost, get out of it.

"Tony comes over daily to feed the horses. I got the house in the divorce settlement, but the horses are his. It's convenient to keep the horses where they have always been — now MY place. Since he comes every day anyway, he picks up his mail there. He has never changed his address. 'Too much trouble,' he said.

"What I really don't like is that when he picks up his mail, he goes through mine. Sometimes he leaves notes on my mail, like, 'What does Jenny have to say?' or 'How come you have a bill from Sears?' I really resent that."

Tony and Shelly haven't made a clean break. They need to.

Zingers

To help yourself make a clean break, don't save up zingers. If during the week you think of zingers, those cute, cutting remarks that will put your ex in place, keep them to yourself. Don't use them when the weekend child visitation swap takes place. Such remarks as, 'I see you've gained some weight,' or 'I don't see how you can buy that new car, knowing how poorly you manage money,' or 'I hear you had a swinging time over the holidays.' These remarks have no place in your frame of recovery, of gaining control of your life. Absolutely nothing is gained by using zingers.

Dropping the Reins

Make a clean break by giving up responsibility for your former spouse. You no longer need to remind your ex to renew a driver's license, buy vitamins or send a Mother's Day card. Let go of the reins. Holding on to them is an excuse for contact, which is no longer appropriate or helpful for recovery.

Fetch 'n Snoop

Don't play games or allow games to be played through your children. Martha told her teenage daughter, "Look through the cabinets when you go visit your father to see if you can find the brass candlesticks. I want them back." Bad game. You can't make a clean break if you send your kids to fetch or snoop.

Snoop 'n Pay

As a matter of fact, you can't play games yourself by snooping and still make a clean break. Carolanne told us in class one week, "I have developed a bad habit of driving by Jackson's house. If I see him leaving I even follow him. I know it's crazy, and I wish I didn't do it. I snoop, thinking I have got to know; then when I find something as a payoff for snooping, I feel worse."

Carolanne was caught up in a game that was not even fun. When the game is not fun, quit playing.

I Can Do It Myself

Carolanne was also showing her inability to respect her former mate's independence. You have to respect that independence and demand it for yourself. You have to realize that the former spouse has a right to privacy, as do your friends.

That also means having the right to independent decisions. Your former mate has the right to make decisions about major purchases — whether wise or foolish purchases — the right to choose vehicles, new friends, new hair style or color, etc.

The reverse is true, too. You have a right to privacy. You have a right to make independent decisions, without having to justify or explain them to your ex. Remember: Just because someone asks you a question doesn't mean you have to answer it. A telephone is a convenience, not a master. You don't have to answer it just because it rings. And you have the option of hanging up or being too busy to talk. *You* have to control the amount of privacy you need.

20 Questions

As you let go and grant that independence, you no longer have a need to question your children about your ex's activities. It's not a fair game to ask the children, "Did your dad put a new tape player in her new sports car?" or "Did your mom go out Saturday night?"

The children don't want to get caught up in the middle of your game. Playing "20 Questions" with them makes them suspicious of you and puts them on the defensive.

Bring on the Popcorn

It is also wise to not be defensive or blaming if the visitation parent does not show up at a scheduled time.

Lindy told us, "Gregory plays golf on Friday afternoons. He's supposed to pick up Johnny at 6:00. Often he's very late. Sometimes he doesn't show at all. I always get upset.

"One time I exploded. I called him names and accused him of being irresponsible. Johnny said, 'It's all right, Mom. Let's play cards and eat popcorn.' Then I felt guilty that Johnny had to calm me down. Now we wait till 6:30. If Greg doesn't show, we just say, 'Oh, well, bring on the popcorn.' I don't explode, and Johnny doesn't get upset either."

If this happens, don't make excuses. You are not responsible for their relationship. Also, don't make accusations, because again, that puts the kids on the defensive for the other parent. Instead, have another plan, just in case.

Just the Facts, Please

The final guideline is a most important one — one to be always remembered. In getting along with your former spouse, always keep it businesslike. No emotion, no sneers, no assumptions. Just facts. If you discuss in a businesslike manner whatever you need to discuss, the two of you will get along much better. It may be a long time before you can be neutral enough to talk in any other way. Meanwhile, keep it businesslike.

When you come out of the house of horrors, even the real world seems a little out of focus at first. You may have to stop for a moment and let your life adjust to this once-familiar scene before going on. It will be an unforgettable experience, but one you can walk away from with an accurate reflection of yourself. The distortions will be gone, and the image you NOW see will be clear, smiling and likable.

Divorce Recovery Journal

At this time write in your divorce recovery journal about getting along with your former spouse, particularly about:

1. The biggest struggle I have in dealing with my ex . . .

2. What I need to change to get along better with my ex . . .

9

The Family Express

ail was obviously very nervous during the class discussion on single parenting. Her fingers played with the pleat in her skirt, and her lips quivered as she spoke.

"My kids seem to think I went to court and gave away half my brain. They know I was the one who initiated the divorce proceedings. They don't know who initiated the downfall of the marriage. They don't understand, and I can't tell them.

"I want them to respect their dad. He's still a good father. If I told them the truth, they would never respect him again. I feel as if I have to protect his honor.

"His dishonor doesn't keep him from being a good father and a good influence on them. I feel as if I'm between a rock and a hard place. To insure their respect for him, they lose respect for me, and I have to live with them.

"They put me on a guilt trip all the time, especially over money. Our standard of living has fallen considerably since the divorce. We used to live very comfortably, but now we scrimp. There's never any extra money for anything unessential. The kids are eleven and fifteen and at a 'wanting' stage. I hear, 'I want, I want,' all the time. When I answer, 'Can't have,' they come back with, 'If you hadn't divorced Daddy . . .'

"Too often I give in. I don't want them to be deprived because I got a divorce. They even say to me that I was dumb to divorce a higher income, and that if I had thought of their welfare I would still be with their father. I don't know what to say to them.

"I did think of their welfare. I thought about it constantly. While they were younger, my husband's activities were not so noticeable. But I knew he couldn't fool them when they got to be teenagers. Living apart and having visitation makes it a little easier. I end up protecting the kids, protecting their father, and catching all the flak.

"And talk about flak! Discipline and respect went out the door. I didn't think my husband was the disciplinarian when we were together. I thought we shared equally in it. Now, though, I've lost my touch it seems. I've lost my nerve, I guess. I can't seem to stand up to my own kids anymore. Often what they say to me hurts, but it makes sense too. So, I stand around dumbfounded and at a loss for words, and they end up thinking I'm dumb."

Gail isn't dumb. Her IQ didn't correlate with her previous income. She came to class to learn. She wanted to restore discipline and harmony at home. The communication with other single parents was a venture in that direction because the talking and listening increased her understanding.

To better understand the change that occurred with Gail and her children, think about and understand the typical child's reactions to divorce.

ALL ABOARD!

Divorce is a family affair. It's like a train, in a way — when the engine quits pulling, the whole train stops because the cars are all hooked together. Your children go through many of the same reactions to the divorce that you and your spouse do. They react with shock, denial, anger and guilt, as well as grief, just as you do. They need the freedom to express their anger and work through their grief, their unstrung emotions. They too will experience broken dreams. What makes it so difficult is that everybody is going through these things at the same time, and somebody has to be in control. Since the kids obviously can't be in control, guess who's elected?

Blowing the Whistle

As the "mature" one, the parent, you may have to postpone your expression of anger, or even grief, until an appropriate moment. Not indefinitely, but just until bedtime, or in the morning.

A child's moment of anger usually passes quickly. Watch children as they play. They can be hot-headed and willing to fight with a friend and five minutes later be arm-in-arm buddies again. So, allow the child his expression of anger. It won't last forever. Expressing it as he goes along will prevent the deep-seated anger that builds into bitterness and resentment. It's like the old steam engine that built up a head of steam and then had to blow its whistle to let off steam and keep going.

Chaney, a boy of ten, had always been mild mannered and good natured. About six weeks after his parents separated, he got in a fight with his sister. This was not typical for him. In his rage, he decided to run away from home. So, he did for about five hours. He came back with tear-stained cheeks. His anger had built to an explosion, and his solitude and tears had helped him resolve it, but the heart-to-heart talk when he got back helped the most. Talking is easier on everyone than running away.

While Chaney was a runaway, his sister was home crying. Her crying was not just over the fight with her brother. Like many sisters, she could dismiss this with a "Who cares?" But she just felt sad. In fact, it was her blues that prompted the fight. She wouldn't pay attention to him like she usually did because she had the blahs. With him gone as a runaway, she had an excuse to cry more than usual. By the time he got back, she was ready to dismiss her tears for the time being. She had needed a grieving time.

Chaney and his sister were behaving normally under the circumstances. They were emotional and needed to vent their strong emotions. They weren't concerned about each other at this point, but their concern was focused inward.

The Child's Fare

A child's world begins and ends at his own belly button. Since he thinks the world revolves around him, most of his reactions center around him, too. And since a child's world centers around self, his questions in response to the announcement of divorce center around self. These questions need to be answered, even if they aren't asked.

One of the first questions is, "What's going to happen to me?" At any age a child is anxious about this. Your child may wonder: "Do I have to move?" "Can I keep my hamster?" "Does this mean I don't get to go to college?" "Will I still get a car?" Your child's anxiety will lessen a great deal if his questions are answered.

Blame's Baggage

Since the child's world centers around self, he will also ask, "What did I do wrong?" A child gets blamed for so much that goes wrong — lost books and coats, broken glasses, slammed doors — that he assumes he blew it again. He needs assurance that he is not to blame for the divorce.

The child reasons, "Since I probably caused this, then I can probably fix it." So, often he will make attempts to get Mom and Dad back together again.

Along this line Gail commented, "The kids have gone so far as to invite their father over for dinner when

I wasn't expecting it. I'm trying to make the break, and they're pulling the other direction."

Children want their home intact. Even if it is a bad home, it's all they know in the way of home, and they want it together.

The Abandoned Boxcar

One reason kids want their home together is that they fear abandonment. "If Mom will abandon Dad, or vice-versa, I could be next." So goes the child's reasoning.

These typical concerns of children need to be addressed. If the child is uncommunicative, open up the conversation with, "What worries you the most about our situation?" or "How do you feel about Dad's leaving?"

In the discussion assure the children, "I will not leave you. We'll stick together no matter what. I need you." Give the necessary assurance to dispel their fears of abandonment.

Jumping the Track

Temporarily children's respect for divorcing parents jumps the track. When Gail's children said, "If you hadn't divorced . . ." and "You didn't think about me," they were expressing a temporary diminished respect.

Some children in some choice words even say, "How can you tell me what to do when you can't even get your act together?" Again, they're expressing a loss of respect. Eventually, if you continue to act in a mature, controlled and respectable way through the difficult times, their respect for you will return. It's up to you to regain their confidence and respect, not by stomping your foot and *demanding* it, but *commanding* it through your life.

When Gail said, "Discipline went out the door," she was relating her children's loss of respect and the ensuing loss of discipline. Her manner with them had changed; so, they had changed. Their relationship was not the same. They were off track.

Yet, the children's needs have not changed. Your child needs food, clothing and shelter. He needs to love and be loved. He needs friends, and he needs a right relationship with God. He needs discipline, consistency and respect. Your problem is to provide those needs as a single parent in a time of personal turmoil and tears.

GETTING BACK ON TRACK

To meet the emotional needs of your children, answer their questions. Give a sufficient explanation. A child has a deep need to know *why* this has happened. Give straight answers. Don't beat around the bush and try to protect the child from the truth. They deserve to know the truth.

Repacking Blame's Baggage

Children should be told emphatically that they are not to blame for the divorce. They need this assurance. Even if they don't ask, tell them.

Gail thought about this a lot. She was very uncomfortable with the thought of giving her children straight answers, but she did agree to give it some more consideration. Giving assurance would be a lot easier.

Riding through Disney World

In addition to answers and assurance, children need some consistency to feel that life is natural. They need familiar scenery and comfortable relationships.

You may ask, "How can I be natural when my own world has fallen apart?" You may not be able to be natural, to feel natural, but treat the children in much the same manner as before. They need and want consistency.

The Disney World father is not being natural. Sam said, "I don't know what to do. I want to be natural, but nothing about the situation is comfortable. I live in a crowded studio apartment. There's nothing to do there but watch TV. That's not visiting. To get away, I've gotten into the habit of entertaining my son. Now he's come to expect it, although he's getting tired of it, too.

"Last Saturday I asked Adam, 'What do you want to do today?'

"He said, 'I guess same ole thing. Go to the zoo, go to McDonald's, go to a movie and fall in bed. You got another idea?'

" 'Yes, I do,' I said.

"I knew from the tone of his voice that I needed to do something different. 'Grandma has been wanting some peaches. There's a farm about thirty miles south where we could pick peaches on the halves. Would you like to go pick peaches with me? I don't have time during the week.'

"He really liked the idea. We went and picked peaches. Then we went to my mother's and helped her peel them. This seemed more natural to me. It must have to Adam, too, because when he fell in bed that night, he said, 'Dad, is picking peaches cheaper than the zoo and movie?'

"I told him it was about the same.

"He said, 'I thought if it would save money maybe we could do it again some time.'

"Being natural will take some planning, but the entertainment whirl takes planning, too. I'm trying in the future to save up things we can do together that are more natural. I'm already thinking next time might be a good time to wax the car and polish shoes — major projects around my place. Think it will work?"

Everyone thought it would. Gail realized she, too, needed to be more natural and to be more like she was before, especially to regain some discipline and respect.

Conducting with Common Sense

Ellen told Gail, "I think you're letting your guilt trip interfere with your common sense. You had respect and control before. Surely you can again. Maybe if you get over your guilt, you can be more logical in relating to your kids."

Gail did need to resolve her guilt feelings in order to stand up and be firm in denying her children's unaffordable wants. She also needed to resolve her guilt in order to have commonsense answers when the children accused her of not thinking of them.

Part-time Engineer

In thinking of the children's needs, think of your own, too. The best you can give your child is the best person you can be. You must get yourself together, be emotionally healthy in order to help your children pull themselves together. Disturbed parents have disturbed children.

Fred told us in class, "I don't enjoy my visitation weekends, and neither does Tim. I've even skipped some weekends because I just couldn't face them. I love Tim very much, but it always turns out badly."

"What makes it so bad?" Sherry asked.

"I guess it's because I always cry. Then Tim cries, and he feels bad. I can feel all right all week, but when I pick him up, it tears me up. I know I'm not doing him any favor, but I can't help it. I want to be a father, a good father, but I can't do it part-time."

Other men in class assured him he could. With a great deal of difficulty, they had done it. They told him he was giving in to weakness instead of building strength. Hank told him, "Fred, when you put Tim's needs before your own, you will become stronger. You can do that, at least for a weekend."

Fred definitely needed to take care of his outlook and emotional health before he could give any guidance to his son. A sobbing weekend was not an uplifting experience. Sure, everybody needs their grieving time, but not all the time.

The Missing Engineer

In this discussion, Ron told us, "I know what crying all the time is like. When I was grieving the most, Melanie, my teenage daughter who lives with me, would try to comfort me. It was amusing to hear her say many of the same things her mother had said when I was down. It was the same tone of voice, same expressions. I let this go on, but I began to regret it when I got myself together again. After a few months, I noticed she was being a lot like her mother, taking responsibility beyond her years. And she would try to take care of me, like serving me. I began to feel really awkward about the situation. I got my grief under control and began to exert more independence and force Melanie to be more independent. It has worked out okay now, but for a few months I was in a sweat. I didn't want her thinking at fifteen that she had to be the mother of the house. I wanted her to be a fifteen-year-old."

Others agreed that you cannot force, expect or allow a child to become the missing parent.

Another important guideline regarding the missing parent is to not assume responsibility for the relationship between your former spouse and child. They must develop their own relationship. This means you can't establish their respect for each other either.

Gail put herself in a difficult position by wanting to ensure the children's respect for their father. In reality, that is their business. She can't do it for them. The father is responsible for establishing his relationship of respect, love and camaraderie.

This same guideline is true on the other side of the fence, too. Don't assume responsibility for tearing down their relationship either. If you belittle your former mate, your child will defend your spouse. If you attack, you get a counter-attack; that's how wars start. Truth wins out. You don't need to touch it up or expose it.

Parrish started an emotional discussion when he responded to this guideline. "I have to tell the kids what she's like. She has boyfriends all the time. I don't want them to admire her way of life. You can call it belittling her if you want to. I don't. I call it teaching them the truth. They must know she is a tramp. I tell them so they won't grow up to be like her. I'd be lying if I told them she was a dear lady."

Fred told him, "We said earlier you are not responsible for their relationship. You don't have to give your opinion either way. You don't have to call her a tramp or a dear lady. Let them decide."

"I can't let them decide. I have to teach them."

Fred retorted, "Teach them the concept you want without using her as an example."

"Why, that would be teaching them I love her and approve of her. I can't do that. I don't want them to love her. I have to teach them to hate sin," Parrish came back.

I couldn't keep quiet any longer. "Parrish, the time will come when you want to teach your children the same principles you live by. That is, love the sinner, not the sin. This might be a good place to start practicing that principle."

Parrish may not quit belittling his ex to the children, but as long as he does, they will defend her. Then they will be defending the lifestyle he wants to turn them away from. His approach won't accomplish his purpose.

DESTINATION: RECOVERY

Parrish loved his children and wanted the best for them, but he hadn't resolved his own anger and humiliation enough to put their needs first.

The child needs and wants the love of both parents. Both parents need to focus on this as their goal. It's not an easy task, but it is an attainable goal. Mature, loving parents can rear mature, loving children, even separately.

The child wants this love so much he will turn from the parent who was always there to try to get the love and acceptance of the parent who withholds it or is absent.

When you, as a loving parent, keep a focus on meeting the needs of your child, you'll find that understanding your child's viewpoint becomes easier. When you let love rule, you can be truthful without being judgmental or critical.

Gail thought about this for days. Two weeks later she reported to the divorce recovery class, "I did it. I was honest with the kids about their dad, and it has made a difference. It's made a big difference.

"We sat around the dinner table long after eating and discussed the divorce. I laid my cards on the table, gently. I told them their father made money illegally, that I considered it too immoral for me to live with and that I had wanted to protect them from knowing this.

"They reacted very strongly. They were mad because this was true, and they were mad because they hadn't been told. They were mad at me, then they were mad at their father. We did a lot of crying and talking. It was good for us. Oh, we did talk a lot.

"Several days later, we talked again. I really feel lucky, blessed I should say, because they took the attitude I wanted them to take. We decided that we can accept imperfection in each other, including me and their father, and keep affection.

"What a load off my shoulders! We get along better, discipline isn't lost, for now anyway, and I am so relieved to not be pretending. I feel badly that they know so much at such a young age. I can't help but want to shield them, but I felt worse before, so I guess I can say, I feel better. I know the kids feel better, and that's really important."

THE CABOOSE

The point is this — divorce affects the whole family. You're all hooked together. To get the family back on track and running, after it's been derailed temporarily, takes a lot of honesty, control and pulling together. The children are a vital part of the process of divorce recovery. They must recover along with you for the recovery to be complete. You are the conductor.

Divorce Recovery Journal

In your divorce recovery journal add paragraphs on these topics:

1. Divorcing parents need to provide children with . . .
2. When parents argue, children should . . .
3. Single-parent families are . . .

10

Applying the S Formula

I've been sober four years now. No alcohol whatever, and I am proud of it. I hope none of you ever go through what I've been through. I haven't only had to face the divorce and loss of home and family, I've also had to face my dependency at the same time. My alcoholism has cost me dearly. I have really paid high to get where I am now.

"Alcohol was the cause of the divorce, she said. I don't blame her for giving up on me. I'm surprised she didn't give up sooner. I didn't know life was as bad as it was. My brain was pickled, and I wasn't aware of how things were.

"When I came home to an empty house except for the letter on the floor, I sobered up fast. I don't mean I quit drinking right then; I just mean I began thinking then. Bare rooms and bare walls are a cold reality. It was actually many weeks before I went to AA and really sobered up. I had denied for years that I had a problem. I just kept right on denying.

HALLUCINATING

"Suzanne had pleaded with me, but I didn't listen. In an empty house though, her words echoed from room to room. I thought I was hallucinating at times. I thought sometimes I actually heard her voice come out of the air conditioning ducts."

"Jim," I could hear her say, "you drink too much. Jim, you're drunk again. I can't stand this. Jim, shape up, or I am shipping out."

"These voices echoed from room to room. I couldn't get away. The voices finally drove me to AA . . . and the fact that she really did ship out. I know I could hear her voice at night when I was trying to go to sleep.

"Accepting the divorce was the hardest thing I've ever done. Going to the first AA meeting was the second hardest thing. I just couldn't admit I had a real drinking problem, but I knew an empty house was real.

"I could feel the emptiness. I decided that since this was real, maybe I had better do something. I couldn't stand the emptiness and couldn't stand the thought of a lifetime of emptiness. Drinking didn't make it go away, and if drinking was creating this emptiness, I had to solve the problem that was creating the problem. So I went to AA.

"Week after week I went. It got easier to go. To make a long story short, after months and months of meetings and counseling, my brain started working again. I learned a lot about myself. I learned what I needed to know.

FACING THE MUSIC

"Divorce forced me to face my problem. I started out thinking divorce was my problem. Then I decided drinking was my problem. What I learned was that my lack of self-esteem was the real problem. My lack of self-esteem caused the drinking, and my lack of self-esteem caused the divorce. My lack of self-esteem has caused all my problems. Today I believe lack of self-esteem is at the bottom of all problems people have.

"My counselor really helped me work on my self-esteem. Sobering up was the best thing that ever happened to me. That, by itself, helped my esteem more than anything. At first I thought it was ridiculous: 'Not drinking for a day won't fill up this empty house. There is no cause-and-effect relationship here. What I want is not to have an empty house. An empty stomach won't change that.'

"My mind played tricks on me, too. I then decided, 'I'll prove them wrong. I'll just show them that drinking isn't the problem.' About the fifth day of not drinking, my attitude changed just a little. I began to have some pride in the fact that for five days I had not had anything to drink.

"After two weeks I went around smothering a little giggle. You know, it was that kind of giggle when you sing to yourself, 'I've got a secret.' I thought to myself, 'I am proving they are wrong,' but at the same time, I was thinking to myself, 'Jim, you're still a strong man. You've gone two weeks without drinking. That's strength. That will show 'em.' But, I wasn't sure anymore what I was proving.

CELEBRATION

"Whatever I was proving, I wanted to keep on proving. Days grew into weeks of being sober, and I began to really be proud of myself. As I grew prouder of what I was doing about the drinking, I noticed other things changing in my life. One Friday I looked back over my sales slips and realized I had made more sales that week than I had ever made in any one week. My first thought was, 'This calls for a celebration,' but I stopped cold in my tracks and added, 'a different kind of celebration. What can I do to celebrate?'

"I decided to call my married daughter Erlene and her husband and invite them over for steaks. I hadn't grilled steaks in a long time. They were tickled to come over.

"My house was so empty, I didn't even have a salt shaker. I had to buy salt, pepper, butter, napkins, everything. It was the most I had spent at the grocery store ever, just to grill steaks. But it was a great evening. It was worth it.

"Erlene was pleased with the change in me. She bragged on my sobriety, she bragged on my increased sales, she bragged on the steaks. I went to bed that night feeling better than I had felt in a long time. That night I thought, 'I guess I'm adjusting to this empty house after all. It doesn't feel quite so empty right now.'

"The next day I went around singing "Little Things Mean a Lot" because that's how I was feeling. Little things were adding up to big changes in my life. I didn't think I was happy, but I knew life was giving me glimpses of feeling better. I began to feel picked up."

THE CULPRIT

Feeling "picked up" is a number one problem for divorcees. There's nothing quite like divorce for making you feel thrown to the ground. Lack of self-esteem often precedes the divorce. Low self-esteem nearly always follows the divorce.

Jim hasn't been the only one in divorce recovery class with self-esteem problems. This topic comes up for discussion about as often as anger. It's very common.

Madge's comment one evening was, "Of course self-esteem is a problem. The person who knows me better than anyone else in the world has said, 'I don't love you anymore. I don't want to live with you anymore.' My self-esteem fell lower than a snake's belly."

Without good self-esteem you keep falling down. You get blown over by life. You have to feel good about yourself in order to keep walking tall, to have enough weight in your shoes to stay on the ground. Self-esteem is the anchor that keeps your ship from drifting off course.

Without self-esteem there is no healing. Healing alcoholism requires self-esteem. Healing the emotional pain of divorce requires self-esteem. Many doctors will say self-esteem affects physical healing, too. Seems essential, doesn't it?

Fruit of the Spirit

Self-esteem is essential for receiving abundant life. Galatians 6:22 tells us the fruit of the Spirit is love, joy and peace, among other things. It is recognizing that Spirit in us that shapes our self-esteem. It is that Spirit in us that makes us the image of God. It is, in fact, not *self*-esteem at all, but *God* esteem. It is our opinion of the God within us that shapes our opinion of self. You have to feel good about God to feel good about yourself and then reap the fruit of the Spirit in your life, which is love of self (God in you), the joy of being yourself (the image of God) and at peace with yourself (God himself in you).

There are many benefits to feeling good about yourself that affect every aspect of your life and make a positive cycle. If you feel good about yourself, you get benefits. When you receive the benefits, you feel good about yourself. It's one time that "going around in circles" is helpful.

Productive

One of the benefits of strong self-esteem is being more productive. Being more productive builds stronger self-esteem. When Jim felt better about himself, he made more sales. When he made more sales, he felt better about himself.

Dory described how this cycle had affected her. "When I am working, I keep up with all my work. I work at the plant 40 hours a week, I keep a neat house, a neat yard and neat kids. Then the plant shut down for a month. I felt draggy. During that month my house went to shambles, I couldn't get any work done in the yard. I didn't bother to fix my hair. Then I didn't like not looking good. As soon as I went back to work, I could get more work done. I fixed up again and felt uplifted. This didn't make sense to me."

To help your self-esteem, control your behavior, your productivity. Be productive. There is much satisfaction in work well done. Then the self-esteem falls in line.

Relationships

People with strong self-esteem are more successful in their relationships than those with low self-esteem. Our relationships give meaning to life because they keep out the emptiness.

Again, change your behavior to get your feelings in order. Jim invited his daughter over for steaks. Relating positively with her made his self-esteem rise.

Character

People with strong self-esteem have strong personal character and higher morals than people with low self-esteem. People with strong character and morals also have higher self-esteem.

Jim felt better about himself when he again felt like a man of strength and character. He had jumped on a bandwagon when he "went on the wagon."

THE S FORMULA

How do you develop strong self-esteem when you are feeling your weakest? You make up your mind to work on it by adding the S Formula to your personality.

Specially Me

The first S in the formula is to realize you are special. You are very special. You are a unique wonder, a miracle.

During a discussion of self-esteem, Judy shared with us, "I didn't really begin to feel good again until I began to realize I am special. For years I have felt fat, ugly and dumb, but I'm not. Now I know I am special.

"You see, I believe in the Bible. The Bible says I am a special child of God. Now, God is all-knowing. His opinion really counts. If he thinks I am special, it must be so. His opinion is worth more than my ex-husband's. I decided to go with God's opinion of me. I really am a neat person."

You feel special when you feel loved. You feel loved when you are loving. When you give love, sincerely, it comes back. You give love by developing loving behaviors. Test this theory with a child. You will see it is true.

You also feel special when you feel that you count for something. So, go where you count. In the church you count. You count in other places, too. If you know a great deal about the stock market, or how to play tennis, teach it to someone else. You get the feeling that "I count" when you share your knowledge or when you share something of yourself.

You also feel special when you feel as if you belong somewhere. So, go where you belong. Again, in the church you get the "I belong" feeling, and you do belong. You can get the feeling of belonging in a neighborhood, a community, PTA, anywhere that you put forth an effort and are recognized. You also get a feeling of belonging in close friendships. When you have a buddy, you belong.

To help you develop the I-am-special feeling, write with a felt tip pen or bold crayon on index cards:

> I Am Special
> I Am Loved
> I Do Count
> I Do Belong

Place these cards at strategic points in your house — taped on the bathroom mirror, propped up on your dresser, taped to the washing machine lid. Every time you go to that place, you will be reminded. Feed your subconscious the message you need to hear. It works.

Success or Less

The second part of the formula for building strong self-esteem is success. As you accumulate successes, you feel better about yourself.

Jim was proud of his sales success and his accomplishment of sobriety, for instance.

Make a list of your successes, no matter how small, and think of ways to expand them. You either "go for success or settle for less." With God's Spirit in you, there is certainly no reason to settle for less.

Set and Scratch

Jim set a goal, a major one, and accomplished that goal. He quit drinking. When you accomplish your goals, it is uplifting.

Jamie said, "I have lived my whole life without goals. I didn't know how to begin to set goals. My sister told me to make a list of things to do, then scratch them out as I finished them. That was a beginning for me. I made a list of things to do the next day, then as I did these items, I would scratch them out. Every time I scratched off something, I would think, 'Got that done.'

"At first my list was really simple, like getting kids off to school on time, making beds, picking up in the bathroom or dusting the bookcase. They were just daily things.

"Then I made my list a weekly list. Buy groceries. Do laundry. Vacuum. Write note of encouragement. I read somewhere that if you write down goals you reach them.

"So, next, I wrote down six-month goals, such as change air filters, touch up paint, wax the car. I made the mistake once of writing down 'save money for new TV.' I didn't get anywhere with that one. So I changed it to 'save $25/month toward new TV.' I accomplished that. I really feel as if I'm getting somewhere when I write down goals and get to scratch them off.

"As I began to feel more accomplished, I made my goals more personal. I had a goal to make a new friend. That wasn't something I could scratch out; so I made a rough outline. Under 'Make a New Friend' I wrote:

1. Start conversation with a stranger.
2. Give a compliment.
3. Do something for someone.
4. Give a word of encouragement.

"I did this once a week and checked it off. You just wouldn't believe what a difference it made. I couldn't believe that writing down lists was so effective, but it sure has been."

Strokes for Other Folks

Another step in the self-esteem formula is giving strokes. Cheer up someone else. When you make someone else feel good, you also feel good. Be generous with sincere compliments. This helps you develop a positive attitude and a little sparkle. You can become the spark plug for someone else's esteem, too.

Stay in Control

A really essential element in the formula for self-esteem is to take control of your life. Your life is not like leaves in the wind. It is controllable. Making decisions gives you control. Making decisions is difficult for some people, but as you build your self-esteem, decision making becomes easier.

Discussing pending decisions sometimes makes it easier. Writing down pros and cons, advantages and disadvantages, may make it easier to make decisions. Decisions have to be made. As you make them you feel more in control. Jamie was taking control when she made her lists. It certainly worked for her.

In regard to decisions, Sue bubbled one evening when she announced, "I bought a car. You guys don't realize what a major decision this has been for me. This is the biggest decision I've made on my own. I decided when to buy a car. I studied the financing and made that decision. I shopped for the car and decided which and what.

"This is stepping into an area of life totally new for me. My son said, 'Mom, I'm so proud for you. You really did it all by yourself.' And I did. After doing something so monumental as buying a car, I feel as if I can do anything now. I actually made all the decisions that go into buying a car. I'm a pretty smart cookie now."

Sue's self-esteem skyrocketed by being in control of the decisions.

Service

The next ingredient in the self-esteem formula is service. A servant's heart is a happy heart. Being of service builds your self-esteem and self-respect as nothing else can.

To be of service, get involved. Get involved with people, really involved. People need you. You need people. You have something to offer. You can be involved by being an encourager, by being helpful, by going the extra mile. It won't cost you anything, and the rewards are magnificent.

Look around you. Everyone you see needs a word of encouragement. Everyone needs help. Be the one to meet those needs. Assume that everyone you meet is wearing a sign around his neck that says, "Make me feel important."

To get involved and be of service, go the extra mile. It will be an exhilarating experience for you. Randy and Charles testified to the excitement of going the extra mile. Suzy wanted to plant a garden. She had a tiller, but lacked muscles. She asked Randy and Charles if they would help by tilling her garden area. They agreed to help out. For two evenings Suzy fixed dinner for Randy and Charles, and the men tilled her garden plot.

For the two men it was a dirty, sweaty job. Those guys had new muscles when they finished. They tilled and raked and did a fine job. Suzy got what she wanted — a good garden plot. But you know who benefited the most? Randy and Charles. They talked about it for weeks. Charles told me, "I really enjoyed that gardening."

Randy said, "Boy, it was good to do something for somebody and be appreciated. Suzy really appreciated our work, and we enjoyed it. Living in an apartment, I never get to work outside anymore. I think I got more out of doing that project for her than she got."

These guys went the extra mile for Suzy. Their friendship didn't require tilling a garden, but going the extra mile built a bond for all three of them that they will remember. Doing something you don't get paid for really makes you feel good. That's going the extra mile.

There's an old Indian proverb that says, "When you help someone else row their boat across the lake, you will reach the other shore yourself." That's what helping and being of service is all about.

Sense of Responsibility

Taking responsibility makes you feel good, too. When you really take a sense of responsibility to work with you, you bring home more than a paycheck. You bring home a sense of pride, a renewed self-esteem. It makes you feel needed and capable, which in turn boosts your opinion of yourself. You are living up to the "God-in-you" potential.

Self-Discipline

Jim's self-esteem soared when he established discipline in his life. The willpower and discipline exerted in going to AA paid off for him, as it does for everyone. Making a decision and sticking to it made him feel like a man of strength. You too will take pride in yourself when you make the decision to do whatever is necessary to control you life by self-discipline.

As Jim was preparing to leave one evening, he said, "I didn't know how low I was until I rose. When I took control of my drinking, instead of allowing it to control me, my life turned around. The control, the decision and the discipline all worked together to make my life better. My house doesn't feel empty now, because my life is full. My relationships at work are better, and my relationship with my daughter is great. Gee, it feels good to be alive!"

These eight elements of the S Formula applied in your life will move you miles ahead in the divorce recovery process. Then you can join Jim in saying, "It's great to be alive!"

Divorce Recovery Journal

This is a very special chapter in your divorce recovery journal. Make it special to you so your life can turn around with a strong self-esteem.

List your assets. Make it a long list. List all your good qualities. You have many.

11

Sex: Blessing or Burden?

When I opened the door to meet Joe for a counseling session, I was overwhelmed by his size. He was six feet, four inches tall, plus Western boots, which made him fill up the door frame. I noticed his long arms, long hands and long legs, all in proportion, and totaling up to a mighty tall man.

As we walked on in, I noticed his good posture. Sometimes very tall people walk with a slump. Not Joe. He walked tall. I thought to myself, "He walks proud. I like that."

We talked for over an hour. Joe talked about his divorce. He talked about his ex-wife. He talked about his children.

THE PARADOX

As I listened to Joe talk about the statistics of his life, I began to see a paradox. Although he walked proud, there was a not-so-proud look about him. I believe it was his eyes. They looked blank so much of the time. He gazed into the distance a lot. I listened intently trying to understand the ambiguity I saw.

"When my wife filed for divorce, I went crazy. One day I would sit in a stupor and cry, and the hours dragged. The next day I would be in a rage, an explosion. I would beat the steering wheel and slam doors. Then I would quiet down into a stupor again. This went on for several weeks.

"Then I decided that if I ran off, disappeared into another state, she couldn't get the divorce. So I took off.

I packed a suitcase and started driving west. I didn't know where I was going, and I didn't care. I didn't know how long it would take to get somewhere or when I would stop. I thought as long as I kept going and nobody knew where I was, the divorce was stopped, that she couldn't do it without me. That was nearly eleven years ago.

THE FRANTIC LIFE

"I went to Oregon. Couldn't go any farther. I stayed in Oregon four months. It did delay the divorce for a while. It was there that I began living differently. I discovered women all over again. I dated with a fury. It was a frantic life. I went out every night. I woke up in a different bed every morning, just about. I thought I was getting even with Deb. I thought I was proving to her that she was wrong about me and that she was wrong in trying to get a divorce.

"Then I called my dad, and he said I needed to come back. Deb was getting the divorce anyway, and I would never see my kids again if I didn't come back and work out some visitation arrangement.

FACING THE FACTS

"I still had to think about it before going back. I just couldn't face the facts. I was working some and partying a lot. I had quit crying all the time, but I knew I couldn't live like this for very long. When I decided to go back, I went. I kept the pedal to the floor and drove twenty-six hours straight, only stopping for gas. I wanted to see my kids again, but I sure didn't want the divorce."

"Joe, you have had eleven years to think about your marriage. In looking back what do you think was the bottom-line problem?" I asked.

He gazed at me a long time before he answered. "I guess I would sum it up as I didn't show love. *Then* I thought the problem was sex. *Now* I believe that because I didn't show love I created the sex problem. At the time, though, all I could see was the sex problem. I still have a sex problem.

"Divorce didn't make the problem go away. Divorce just put the same problem in a different frame. Well, actually, the problem is different. Sex is a problem now because of the guilt I live with. I didn't live with sex and guilt when I was married. It was sex and selfishness then. Now it is sex and guilt, and I guess selfishness, too. I don't know . . ."

THE CYCLE

"How was sex a problem when you were married?" I asked. Long pause. We both stared at the floor.

"She wasn't interested. I was. She never seemed to want sex. I would try to get her interested, and wait. When I had waited as long as I could stand, I would force the issue and get my way. Then we would both be mad. She would be mad because I had forced her, and I would be mad because it had come to that.

"Then I would make up my mind not to force her again. But the cycle just repeated. I would wait longer and longer, sometimes months. Sometimes Deb slept on the couch; sometimes I did. It was really a bad scene.

"I still have a problem with sex. I don't wait for months anymore. I made up my mind while I was in Oregon I would never go through that kind of agony again. So, for a few years I was a real swinger, or so I thought. But the fun left me, and I began to go through periods of disgust. I've changed from liking women to being disgusted by them. But, I'm beginning to realize that women probably haven't changed. I have. And maybe what I am disgusted with is myself, and not women.

"At first I thought I was getting even with Deb. Every time a woman would enjoy being with me, I thought to myself, 'See, Deb, you had it all wrong. Other women enjoy being with me.' I thought I was proving something to her. It was a long time before I realized Deb didn't care. She didn't even know what I was proving; so, it meant nothing to her. Then I asked myself, 'What am I proving?' I haven't come up with an answer.

"This much I do know. I can go to bed with a woman and be excited. Then I wake up the next morning and think, 'How could she have been exciting? She is disgusting. Any woman that would let me use her like this isn't worth a plug nickel.' But it really is me I'm disgusted with. I can look back on some experiences and realize that they weren't disgusting. I was disgusting.

"So I get on a cycle of wanting to straighten out my life. I live celibate for a while and try to associate with a better group of people. I go to, say a church singles' function, and I feel as if I don't fit. I think to myself, 'If these people knew how I live behind closed doors, they wouldn't be so friendly to me.' I put on an act of trying to be like them, and that doesn't fit. Then I rebel and withdraw from them and go back to my partying, and that makes me feel bad. I'm really a mess, and I don't know what to do about it. I know one thing though. I'm not going to drop out of the church. The church is too important. I absolutely couldn't live with myself if I quit. I'm glad my dad embedded my brain with, 'Never miss going to church.'

"But I don't fit. Sometimes I think, 'They're a bunch of phonies. They probably live just like me.' Then I think, 'No, they may not be innocent, but they don't live like me. They have a better grip on life than I do.' I've got to get a better grip on life, too. My cycles are driving me bananas. My roller coaster ride is not fun anymore. Too much of the time I can't stand myself. I can't stand other people either, especially women, and I can't stand the loneliness.

"I withdraw from people thinking my isolation is the answer. Then I can't stand that, and I go to the other extreme. What I would give for a good solid middle-of-the-road life."

After many hours of soul-searching over the following months Joe began to realize that his promiscuity was not just a sexual problem but a self-esteem problem. By living a life of degradation, he was feeling so low he couldn't stand himself anymore. He called it disgust. His problems had to be addressed, and Joe began the slow process of divorce recovery first by taking responsibility for his actions. To take responsibility for his actions, he first had to understand the truth and consequences of sex.

TRUTH AND CONSEQUENCES

Do you remember the old TV show "Truth or Consequences"? Jack Linkletter asked the contestant some impossible-to-answer question, and the contestant made a wild guess, which was always wrong. Then the contestant had to suffer the consequences for his wrong answer, which was some ridiculous and embarrassing prank the show had dreamed up — a pie in the face, a bucket of water over the head, etc. It was great for a few laughs.

Unfortunately, the consequences for wrong answers about sex are no laughing matter. And newly divorced people like Joe often have impossible-to-answer questions about their sexuality now that they're single again:

"Just because my ex was a jerk and walked out on me, does that mean I have to go without sex for the rest of my life?"

"How far is too far? As long as there's no actual intercourse, can't we fool around all we want?"

"The Bible doesn't talk about masturbation. Does that mean there's no limit to my activity in that area to have some kind of relief?"

Tough questions. And no absolutely-right-in-every-situation answers. The truth is, all a single-again person can do is select his best answer, based on what God's word does say, and considering the consequences.

The Truth

The truth is, some answers have more damaging consequences than others. Some single-again people come up with wrong answers and misuse their sexuality, thinking it will make their life better in some way, seeking revenge and retaliation, or acting out their anger as Joe did. Here are misuses of sex to watch out for.

Recreational Sex. "If it feels good, do it." That's how some people react. They use sex for their personal recreation or fun, with little or no consideration for the other person. But, nobody likes to be used, and nobody feels good about himself when he uses others. By using others, you lose respect for them and for yourself. Then, instead of reducing loneliness, it's increased, because without respect for others, there is no one to relate to.

Ego Booster. Some people enter sexual encounters thinking, "This proves I am masculine/feminine/attractive/desirable." They use sex as an ego booster. The idea of an attractive sex partner or, as Joe put it, seducing "top quality," sounds like a real emotional "upper." They are living for the moment with little thought to the consequences.

Acting Out Anger. After a divorce or broken relationship, frustration and anger usually run very deep. Frustration and anger are both active, strong emotions, and strong emotions tend to increase sexual desire. Unfortunately, some people put those strong emotions into sexual action and take out their anger and frustration on a new sexual partner, subconsciously believing that they are expressing their anger to their former mate. It's a type of substitution — they substitute a new person into the place of their former mate in order to take out their angry frustration.

Revenge or Retaliation. Some people try to "get even" with their former mates by sexual encounters with new partners. "If he could only see me now, he'd be sorry for what he did to me." Or, "I'll show her!" This again is a type of substitution. It's like punishing your son for something your daughter did because your daughter's not at home, and he's available. Joe finally realized that he was only hurting himself because his ex did not feel the effects of his revenge.

The Consequences

These misuses of sex are not the best answers, and the participants will probably suffer consequences, such as these:

Guilt. It felt good at the time, but now that it's over the guilties set in: "I shouldn't have done it. I knew it was wrong." "It's all my fault; I could have said no." "God, please forgive me. I know I don't deserve it; I'm a really rotten person."

Guilt occupies your mind. It's like a whirlwind that goes round and round inside your head. It causes you to lie awake at night condemning yourself. And, perhaps, that's not all bad, if it causes you to change your ways and turn back to God. The fact is, misuse of your sexuality is wrong, and you know it; so your conscience gives you a working over, as it has been trained to do. Be thankful to God that his Spirit lives within you and guides you back to him, even through guilt.

Low self-esteem. Your ego probably took a real blow when you got divorced, for whatever reason. Your sexuality may have been battered and bruised. So, you may have thought a sexual experience would renew your sexual self-image. It would give your ego a boost and restore your sexual confidence. And, as Joe found out, the experience itself may have been exhilarating, exciting . . . for the moment. Now that it's a memory, though, the guilties have taken over, reality has set in, and you're disgusted with yourself. Instead of an ego *boost*, it was an ego *bust*. You actually accomplished just the opposite of your goal. And the more often you participate, the lower your self-esteem dips. It's a downward spiral. It's a part of God's plan for people to feel good when they do right and to feel badly when they do wrong so they will turn back to the right.

Depression. The guilties and low self-esteem, along with the knowledge that you're being promiscuous, often cause depression. You get the blahs, and then the blues. Some single-again people become so depressed from unfulfilling sexual relations that it just doesn't seem like life's worth living anymore. Some even commit suicide over it.

Fatal consequences. There are other consequences, too, which result from misuse of sex. Some people lose their jobs due to sexual misbehavior at work. Some lose their friends who no longer wish to associate with an immoral person. Some turn to alcohol or drugs due to depression. Some end up with unwanted pregnancies and diseases, such as AIDS, or go to prison due to sex crimes. The truth is, the consequences are anything but laughable. They can be, in fact, terminal — emotionally, physically, socially and spiritually.

THE REAL PROBLEM

As Joe discovered, the real problem is usually not sex at all. Sexual difficulties are often only the symptom of the real problem. The root problem is most often poor self-esteem or lack of self-love, which manifests itself in various ways.

Sex is intended to be an expression of committed love and the desire to help the other person reach his fullest potential and happiness in life. But you can only love someone else as much as you love yourself. Joe said his real problem was that he didn't "show love" to his wife. In reality, Joe's still one step short of the truth. He didn't love himself and, therefore, he *couldn't* show love to his wife. And because she didn't receive committed love and care, she didn't want empty, meaningless sex.

You see, the real problem was Joe's self-esteem, not sex. Saying, "We have a sex problem," is like saying, "I have a cough." You really have a bad cold that causes your cough. You can't cure the cough by eating candy cough drops; you have to take medicine that attacks the cold itself. And you can't solve your sex problems without attacking the real problem, which is usually self-esteem in one of its disguises.

Immaturity

One mask that poor self-esteem wears is immaturity. For instance, one sexual partner may have set opinions about "proper" sexual techniques, proper times for sex or proper places for sex, with no tolerance for the other partner's more flexible views. This mindset is a mark of immaturity. A mature person recognizes that people from different backgrounds will naturally have different ideas about these things, and they are not threatened by those ideas. The mature person's self-esteem is positive enough to allow freedom of thought and feeling to others. The immature person's self-esteem is not full-grown and may not allow that freedom. Immature persons are not risk takers. They only do what feels "safe" to them. This lack of flexibility in an intimate relationship can definitely cause sex problems. But the real problem is adolescent self-esteem, expressing itself as immaturity.

Selfishness

At the heart of many problems in close relationships, including sex, is selfishness. "I'm not in the mood," or forcing the issue as Joe did are examples. It is the practice or nonpractice of sex with little or no consideration for the needs or desires of the other partner. "I have a headache" is a standing joke about selfishness in sex, but it's not as funny in the bedroom as it is in a crowd.

Selfishness is another expression of poor self-esteem. Strong self-esteem allows a person to develop a giving attitude, to put the other person's needs above self. It is outwardly focused. Poor self-esteem is inwardly focused. It is occupied with self and making self feel good.

Selfishness can cause two extremes in sex — too much or too little. It can cause boredom or fear. It can cause frustration and ruin intimacy. But, once again, it's not sex that's the problem; it's the lack of self-love disguised as selfishness.

Inequality

Another costume in which poor self-esteem parades through the bedroom is inequality. The person who does not love self either dominates others or allows others to dominate him. He/she may overcompensate for the lack of self-esteem by acting highly confident, or he/she may bow and scrape to the other person's every whim. When this dominance or subservience enters a sexual relationship, intimacy walks out. All chance for vulnerability, closeness and sharing have been squelched. Equality allows openness without condemnation. It gives the freedom to express deep feelings either physically or verbally.

It is man and woman together who are created in the image of God. "God created *man* in his image. Male and female created he them." They are equal parts of God's image, complementing each other, completing each other. That's why you often hear the question, "Hey, where's your other half?"

Inequality can cause major sex problems in a relationship, but inequality, too, is only a cover-up for wavering, weak self-love.

This basic problem of poor self-esteem blocks the path to the treasure of sexuality. It stands between you and the gift of sex that God intended.

THE GIFT OF SEX

God gave the gift of sex so man could share *intimacy*. All gifts have a cost. The cost of this gift is commitment. You determine if the gift is a blessing or a burden. In its intended context, it's a blessing; out of context, it's a burden.

To assure that future relationships are meaningful and according to God's plan, study the ladder of relationships on the next page and how the relationship progresses.

Building relationships is like climbing a ladder. When I climb a ladder, and I often do, I go one step at a time. Any other method is dangerous. To skip steps makes the ladder unstable. I've never bought a ladder with one rung missing, and I wouldn't want one like that.

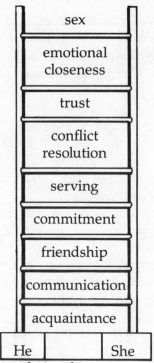

In building a relationship, too much too soon, or trying to jump ahead to sex by skipping the other important steps in the ladder, causes a shaky feeling. It makes you insecure. To skip a rung keeps the relationship from progressing steadily upward. The fall can be harmful. The best method is to take all the fundamental steps, each one building on the previous one, until sex can be a natural expression of commitment, trust and love.

One of the themes of the Song of Solomon is repeated often in the book, such as chapter two, verse seven. The paraphrased idea there is, "Don't get sexual before it's time." When you jump ahead to sex in a relationship, you break this principle of God for developing happy, permanent commitments.

The old *King James Version* used the words "to know" when it described the sexual relations between two people. Satan lies to our society by saying that the best way "to know" another person is through sex: "If it feels good, do it." "How can it be wrong if it feels so right?" "Let's get physical."

The real struggle with sexuality for single-again people is to try to put sexuality back into God's framework. Joe was right when he said divorce put sex problems into a different frame. In this case, it was still the wrong frame. It was still out of focus, and the picture was blurred.

Joe learned the cost of promiscuity was too high. He was attempting to find intimacy. Real intimacy is not only physical, but also emotional and spiritual. In fact, without the emotional commitment, there is no real intimacy in sex, as demonstrated in the relationship ladder. And without God in the relationship, the sweetest intimacy of all is missed.

Joe was hiding his emotional self. He hid his emotions of anger, guilt, fear and shame. Consequently, by not being emotionally known by his changing sexual partner, he could not obtain his goal of intimacy. He wanted to ease his loneliness, anger and pain. What he got instead was more isolation, loneliness and added anger.

It was a long struggle to solve the esteem problem that caused the sex problem for Joe. The guilt and bad feelings lasted so much longer than the pleasure that it was not worth the cost. The fact is, you can't take something created for one purpose and use it in another way and expect it to work. It's like trying to use a hammer when you really need a paint brush. It just won't work.

Expression of Love

The purpose of sex, in addition to obtaining intimacy, is to express love. Love is giving, not taking. The reward in taking is momentary; the reward in giving is eternal.

Expressing pretended or false love through promiscuous sex produces only false and guilt-ridden pleasure that vanishes with the dawn. Only the love of total emotional and physical commitment fulfills the purpose of sex as God designed it and results in his promise of peace and commitment for life.

That's easy enough to say, and even believe. But it's a lot harder to live with when you're single-again and alone and vulnerable. Staying pure doesn't always have nearly as much appeal as sex.

True enough. Single-again sexuality can be a real burden to a Christian. The solution is to turn the burden into a blessing.

THE BLESSING OF CLOSENESS

Sex isn't all there is to life. Sex is only one part of a relationship. Granted, it's an important part, but without the closeness built into a relationship first, it's a meaningless part. Our society puts far too much emphasis on sex, and as a result, Americans have become enslaved to the "glamour of sex." In fact, sex has become a type of god that we worship . . . falsely.

Intimacy and closeness are really what make life sweet. Intimate communication and sharing all of life with people soften the blows of life and cushion our disappointments. And that's where the single can count blessings galore!

The freedom of singleness allows the development of many close friendships. Because a single or single-again person is not tied to only one other person, the doors are open to step out and make new friends, form new relationships, chase dreams, take on extra responsibility and spend more time with God. And because singles have more time to dedicate to new relationships, they can be blessed with closeness and intimacy with several others.

Authenticity

Emotional closeness in friendship is begun and nurtured through being authentic. When you are the real you, not the disguised you, you will be appreciated for your lack of phoniness, for honesty, for vulnerability.

This closeness comes through give-and-take communication. Talking and listening both build intimacy and closeness, ultimately leading to healthy relationships. These close friendships help satisfy our need to belong and not be isolated. They lift our burdens and bless our lives.

Affirmation

Divorcees also need affirmation. Married folk do, too. If you give affirmation to others, you affirm yourself. It always comes back to you. You can sincerely say more often to people, "You're neat," "I appreciate you," "I admire you." That's affirmation. "I am glad you're dependable." That's affirmation. "I'm glad we're friends. I love you." Affirmation leads to closeness and intimacy.

Affection

The same is true of affection. If you give affection, you get more affection. The giving and receiving of affection has a long-lasting effect on your well-being. Nonsexual hugs are affection, as are pats on the back, "holy kisses" and smiles. A sincere smile and sparkle in the eye give affection. Affection builds closeness and a sense of belonging.

Sometimes you have to *learn* how to be more affectionate and warm, especially if you were raised in a less affectionate environment as a child. If your family didn't hug much, it probably feels a bit awkward at first to hug even your closest friends. You may find that if you try it a few times it will get easier.

CURBING THE PROBLEM

One of the most difficult times to deal successfully with your sexuality as a single-again, of course, is in a dating situation. This is not new. It's the same kind of difficulty you faced before you were married. And, should you decide to date again, the experience will probably be similar. Here are some suggestions to help curb the problems. Not any one of these will work for everyone. That's because each person is different. Hopefully, you will find one or two on this list that you may want to incorporate into your routine that will help.

1. *Set your limits.* Before you go out, mentally (and even in writing for emphasis) set your own limits so as not to violate your conscience and God's word. If you don't *set* limits, you will *have* no limits. That's when the trouble starts.

2. *Group date.* Instead of putting yourself into the more intimate setting of one-to-one dating, go out with other couples or with a group of singles. There's safety in numbers usually. It's a good way to get to know someone and decide whether you want to be alone with him.

3. *Pace your dating.* As Jim Talley and Bobby Reed point out in their excellent book *Too Close Too Soon* (Thomas Nelson Publishers), too much time together too soon causes familiarity and intimacy problems. Just simply say no sometimes to going out. Give yourself the time and space you need to be logical about a relationship, whether it's romance or friendship.

4. *Set a curfew for yourself.* People are most vulnerable late at night. Give yourself an "out" by setting a time to be home. You don't have to stay out unless you want to. Just say, "I'd love to go with you, and I'll need to be home by eleven." Dates that do not have a planned end are traps set to spring, whether intentional or not.

5. *Keep your guard up.* There are other vulnerable times, too, especially for a divorced person. Holidays, anniversary dates, birthdays or when you're really tired are times to keep your personal guard up. Make a list of the times when you consider yourself most vulnerable. Then circle them on your personal calendar as a reminder to yourself to be careful during those times.

6. *Guard what you read and watch.* Research has proven time and again that people are definitely affected by the books and literature they read, as well as the TV shows and movies they watch. It is a form of mind programming and brainwashing that has been approved by society, but not by God. His word says, "Whatever is true, whatever is noble, whatever is right, whatever is pure, whatever is lovely, whatever is admirable — if anything is excellent or praiseworthy — think about *these* things" (Philippians 4:8). We become what we think about. So, if you read sexually stimulating books and watch sensual movies and shows, controlling your sexuality will only be more difficult for you.

7. *Plan wholesome activities.* Don't let a date "just happen," because often the wrong kinds of things end up happening, even when it's unintended. Instead, plan your activities so they are proper and less "dangerous" to your vulnerability.

8. *Measure quality.* It is inevitable that whoever you marry will be someone you date. So, it's important that you try to measure the quality of the person you date. That's not to say you are being spiritually judgmental, but you do have to decide if a person you date is the one with whom you want spend the rest of your life. Spirituality is at the top of the list; then make your own list from there on of the qualities that are important to you. *Bottom line:* Don't date someone who does not possess the quality you're looking for. It's a setup for disaster.

9. **Feed on the word.** This is your source of strength in times of temptation and depression. These are the words of gentle reminder about your standards and the qualities to search for. These are the words of your Father who loves you and wants you to be happy. You are never alone when you're with your Father in his word.

10. *Pray after each date.* Make it a regular part of your dating pattern. When you know that you'll be talking to the Father at the end of your time together, it will warn you not to do what you don't want to have to confess. This may sound strange at first, but those who have tried it recommend it highly.

WALKING PROUD

Controlling your sexuality as a single-again person is no easy matter. It's a part of you that needs to be expressed, in one way or another. Like forgiveness, sexual purity is a decision that must be made over and over. It's a decision that may require change of heart and mind and actions. But it's a decision that allows your self-esteem to rise steadily. It's a decision that helps you to lift your head up and walk proud.

Brad told our class one evening, "I thought I could play with sexual dynamite and be safe. I found out I couldn't. I had to quit the locker room joking. I had to quit buying 'skin' magazines. I had to change." He had more control of his thoughts after he consciously controlled his behavior.

Brad and Joe reported months later a side benefit to the behavioral changes in their lives. They said they had become more sensitive to the hurts, needs and feelings of others.

Joe's final comment to me months later was, "I made the decision, but I have failed. I didn't let it get me down, though. I had to redecide. I've had to reprogram my way of thinking. I've worried, agonized, argued, resisted, cried and cried some more for hours, days, even years. After all this, I have finally changed my lifestyle. Through persistence in following through, I now have control over that part of my life that did have control over me.

"The change in me is tremendous. I like everybody better now that I like myself better. Now I get to the bottom of it all, and it's so simple: DON'T."

As he walked off I thought to myself, "There goes a man who walks tall. He walks proud, too."

Divorce Recovery Journal

This journal assignment will be beneficial for a long time. Write out honestly to yourself a page about "the trouble I have with my sexuality . . ."

Explore your "problem behind the problem." Before you finish this journal assignment, also write at least a paragraph answer to each of these two questions:

1. What is the moral standard I want my children to live by? For me to live by?

2. What can I do during the next thirty days to have more control in my life?

12

Too Guarded to Love

The best one-word description of Valerie might have been *arrogant* the first time she came to divorce recovery class. The second choice one-word description might have been *opinionated*. She was certainly strong in her opinions when she first talked about love.

"I loved my husband. He didn't think I did, but I did. He used to tell me I was too guarded to love. I still don't understand why he said that. I *was* guarded, and I would tell him he was too, as everyone is. He wouldn't admit it, but I know it's true.

"Everyone has to be self-protective, or we would be crying all the time. I don't intend to ever be off guard. If I let my guard down, people take advantage of me. To let people run over me is dumb. If letting people run over me is showing love, I won't ever show love. I loved him, but I wouldn't let him push me around.

"Now I think of love like eating raw oysters. I tried it once, and I didn't like it. Why try it again? Raw oysters are hard to swallow. I can get my vitamins some other way."

TESTING TRUST

Bruce was quick with his comeback to Valerie. "Sounds to me like you don't trust people. I think it's quite normal not to trust people after a divorce, for a while, but you sound as if maybe you never have trusted and have made up your mind never to trust people. Are you sure that's how you want to be?"

"I trust people," she said. "I trusted my husband. I never accused him of cheating on me. I trust you."

Bruce said, "Would you loan me ten dollars? We don't really know each other well, but I need ten dollars. How 'bout it?"

"Sure, I'll loan you ten dollars," she answered.

"Well," Bruce slowly said, "Let's suppose you are well off, better than average, and what I really need is a hundred dollars, and you can spare the hundred. Would you loan me a hundred dollars?"

Valerie laughed. "No, I wouldn't loan you a hundred dollars. But I don't consider that a test of trust. That's a test of how dumb am I. If you need a hundred dollars, you probably wouldn't come up with a hundred dollars to pay me back. It's easier to come up with ten dollars to give me, but a hundred dollars? Besides, if you didn't pay me back, ten dollars isn't much to lose."

Bruce retorted, "I think we *could* call this a test of trust. I think what you are saying is that you don't trust people, and because you don't trust people, you don't want to love. You're not alone here though. I've wrestled with this myself. I know others have, too. My trust was violated in my divorce, and I felt just like you and said, 'I'll never love another woman.' I stuck with this decision for a long time. I guess you could say this attitude protected me till my pain went away.

A NEW MEANING

"Gradually, it dawned on me that I wasn't as happy as I could be. I was becoming bitter, and I was quick to think I disliked, even hated, a lot of people.

"I heard a sermon on trust that gave me new thoughts. It was about trusting God. Oh, I had heard the words before, but they took on a new meaning this time. You've probably heard, 'You hear what you're ready to hear.' Well, I suppose I was ready to hear something with a new meaning for me.

"I put together a string of thoughts. Distrust falls in the same category of feelings as hate and bitterness. I wanted to be happier. To become happier I was going to have to get on the other side of the fence with words such as trust and love. Climbing that fence hasn't been easy, but I decided to give it a try. If I didn't like it, I could go back to my old ways.

"People laugh and think I'm joking when I say now that I can fall in love every thirty days, and in a way I am joking, but in a way I'm not. What I mean is that I'm trusting enough now to be susceptible to falling in love every thirty days, given the opportunity. I'm not really that flippant about falling in love, but I am that trusting now, and I'm certainly happier."

Bruce continued with, "I certainly would like to see you get to the same place I am. Valerie, it could be that lack of trust prevents love in your life. Every thirty days isn't a bad idea."

DISTRUST DISASTERS

I don't know about falling in love every thirty days, but Bruce is right about what lack of trust can do. It's disastrous. It can prevent happiness and love. Distrust can lead to hate and bitterness.

Failing Friendship

Lack of trust for people prevents friendships or causes them to fail. To be friends, we have to trust each other. I have to know that you're not going to stab me in the back. I have to know you're going to stand by me. I have to know you'll defend me, keep my secrets and be there when I need you. And you need the same from me for us to be friends. This trust is the basis for the kind of friendships we want. We can't give each other written guarantees for all the ways we will treat each other; so, we simply have to go on trust.

Left Behind

Thinking of going on trust reminds me of an incident that happened on a vacation. On one of the singles' backpack trips in Colorado, fifteen of us came to a log crossing which was over swift water and a rocky creek bed. The two-log crossing was slippery and wobbly — in fact, very wobbly. It was frightening to all of us weak-kneed, inexperienced wilderness wanderers.

Jim Withers and I crossed over to the other side and took off our backpacks. Then we returned to help each person get across the logs. One of us would carry a backpack over, and the other would steady and walk with the person across those wobbly logs.

Afterwards I thought, "Those people trusted Jim and me to get them across those logs. There was absolutely no reason for them to trust us. We were just as inexperienced as they were. Why did they trust us?"

The answer I came up with was that they trusted us because they thought the alternative was to get left behind. Life is like that log crossing. We either trust, or we get left behind.

Nothing to Lose

The backpackers may also have thought that they had nothing to lose by trusting us. This "nothing to lose" attitude was what Bruce took when he decided to trust and love again. He was unhappy hating people. He reasoned that he wasn't going to be unhappier by loving. And the potential could be rewarding.

Everything to Gain with God

The potential for happiness is available and rewarding when you shift your trust. In marriage you had trusted your spouse at one time. You trusted your mate to consider your welfare, to provide your needs, to be there. You placed trust in your dream. Now you need to shift your trust from a person to God. When you put your trust in God, it's also easier to trust your fellow-man.

When your trust is in God, you know that he will be there. With that added strength, if a person isn't there, you can still go on with life. This keeps us from always falling down in difficult times.

When your trust is in God, you can know he will consider your welfare. You will not be hurt beyond endurance. You will be given answers, and you will receive blessings.

When you place your trust in God, you know he will provide for you. Valerie couldn't loan Bruce the hundred dollars because she didn't trust that she would get it back. In trusting God, it doesn't matter what Bruce does, because somebody bigger and better than Bruce is in charge and will take care of the situation. This isn't silly. It's smart — even wise.

Move toward People

This shift in trust enables you to move toward people and not away from people. The lack of trust leaves you alone, isolated, moving away and left behind. It also prevents the divorce recovery that is possible through trust.

Trusting brings you closer to people. Your satisfaction with life is your satisfaction with how you relate to people. You can't be happy going it totally alone for long. You've got to trust somebody.

For a renewed trust in people, renew your trust in God.

THE TRUST TRAIL

Trust can't be restored overnight, nor the ability to trust again. It's a little-by-little process. The key is to start. Test it. Put a little bit of trust in someone. It begins with a decision.

Hitting the Trail

To renew trust is a conscious decision. Bruce made the decision. He acted on the decision to trust and liked the result. He called those results "falling in love every thirty days." Maybe everybody doesn't understand when he jokes about it, but it sounds good to me. The point is, you have to hit the trail back to trust sometime, but you're the one who has to decide to get started.

That decision, though, is not once and for all. The decision to trust must be made over and over, with each new person, each new friendship. You can, however, develop the habit of making a positive decision for trust by trusting a little bit, then a little more, then a lot. It's a progressive, graduating decision process.

Happy Trails

Trust is the key to love, and love is the key to happiness. Moreover, you, as a single, can be loved and be loving again.

One way of being loved is to be known. You are unique and special. When you let yourself be known, you'll be appreciated and loved. You can be known by expressing your hopes, your thoughts and your feelings, your dreams.

Valerie was letting herself be known when she added to the discussion, "I hear what's being said. Bruce, you make sense, but right now I'm afraid. I'm not sure. I'm afraid not to be self-protective. I've always had to take care of me. I believe your change worked for you, but I'm not so sure about me."

She was letting her fears show, and we appreciated her new vulnerability. She received understanding and appreciation by letting herself be known. She even got more hugs when class was over that night. She had, perhaps unconsciously, stepped onto the trail back to trust.

Love Tokens

Besides letting yourself be known, another way to get love is by giving love. Call it love tokens.

You carry with you at all times a handful of love tokens. Deposit a token in somebody else's cup. When you go around giving out your tokens, tokens come back to you. You'll never run out. If you deposit a token in someone's cup and don't get one back, that isn't important. The problem may be with that person, not with you. That person's cup may be so empty he has none to return. So give another. He needs it. By doing this, you will get deposits in your cup from somewhere else.

By dropping love tokens along the way, you may leave a trail back to trust that another hurting person can follow, too. This is similar to the story of Hansel and Gretel. They left a breadcrumb trail in order to find their way home. By leaving a love token trail, you and others find your way back to a more comfortable, "at home" feeling.

Face Value

You can accept the occasional lack of token returns because you know your cup is full. In fact, it will run over when you accept another person at face value. You want to be accepted and will be when you accept others.

Being able to accept others as they are is based on your knowing that God accepts you as you are, that he was willing to give his only son to stand in your place *because* of what you are. He loves you, warts and all. So, you can love others through him, warts and all.

Love Commits

Love is a commitment to a way of life. When you love, you commit yourself to loving behavior and acceptance toward others. Loving behavior and acceptance are not based on a condition. To say, "I love you if you measure up to my expectation" is not expressing love. That's making demands.

For instance, parental love is a decision, a commitment and acceptance without conditions. If your child comes in long faced and anxious about his report card because of an F in geometry, you don't say, "Well, that's it. Yesterday I loved you, but now? Look at this. An F on your report card. Go pack your things and find another home. I don't love you anymore."

No, you don't react like that because your love for your child is not based on conditions of excellence. You may not approve of the grade, but you still love the person. You can't help but love. You have already made the decision and commitment to love the child, and the condition doesn't change that.

This same type of commitment and acceptance is what is needed in your other relationships with people. Love them as you love your children, because they are God's children.

Love Attracts

As you reflect the loving attitude of acceptance and not conditions, you attract loving people. People are attracted to your loving behavior, reactions and acceptance.

As you increase your understanding and acceptance of yourself, your reactions to others change, too. As you control the changes in your life, your personal life improves. You move from bitterness and hate toward acceptance and love.

HEALTHY LOVE

Your personal life improves because your love spills over to others when your self-love is adequate.

Often divorcees feel so unworthy at the beginning of the divorce process that self-love hits an all-time low.

At this point, relationships are based on need. Need relationships are not long-lasting ones. Needs change, thankfully. However, at the beginning of this crisis point, you may feel a "need to be needed" in order to feel worthy again.

Discussing this, Madge smiled and said, "I know about these need relationships. My husband had been such an aggressive, hostile, temperamental man, I was exhausted when our divorce was final. The first man I dated was really laid back. I needed that change. He was very even tempered, calm in all situations, and I thought it was wonderful. After a few months though, I began to realize that he was so laid back that he was only one level above sleep. I didn't need that on a long-term basis. I could get restless quickly on a steady diet of very laid back. My need changed, but the relationship met a temporary need and really helped me build my self-esteem at that time."

As your evaluation of self-worth bounces back, you can base relationships on want. "I want to love you," "I want to be your friend," and "I want to share a part of life with you" make far better relationships than ones based on need.

Your self-love is so important, because you can only love others as much as you love yourself. How you love others is a reflection of your self-esteem. How you love others reflects who you are and how you love God.

You act loving to others by learning to trust and by showing loving behaviors. Then your reflection will glow as never before.

Valerie laughed as the class was closing, and she told us, 'Bruce, you said you hear what you need to hear. I can accept the fact that I needed to hear this discussion, but I'm not sure yet I can make the changes you did. I'll bring a hundred dollars with me next week, just in case. But don't make out a deposit slip."

We all laughed at this bit of humor. We loved Valerie for her honesty and accepted her where she was. There was hope for her. She wants to recover and not be bitter and hating. She would learn to trust and love again. She was definitely on the right trail. And she was letting her guard down a little at a time.

Divorce Recovery Journal

Don't let the "Yes, but . . ." keep you from developing love and trust. To help you, in your divorce recovery journal respond to the following:

1. What I am doing now to make myself more loving is . . .

2. The attitudes I need to change, to become more accepting of others are . . .

3. Perceptions I can change that will make me more trusting are . . .

4. What I will do to increase self-love is . . .

13

Opening Pandora's Box

I'm a survivor. It's been tough, but I feel as if I've made it. Divorce really threw me to the bottom, but I've bounced back. Now I'm happy, but I still want to share life with people. I've made mistakes, and I've learned from them. I want to move on to something else."

Geneva spoke with a sparkle as she went on, "I've dated, mostly very casual dating, nothing serious, but I want more, and I don't know how to get there. I don't know how to get to a deeper emotional level. I don't know what keeps me from getting to more serious dating. Fear maybe?

"When I think about what can happen, it's frightening. But I think I'm smarter now. I have to be. I've gone through too much not to be smarter. I'm confident of not repeating my mistakes. Yes, I want to relate better."

When Geneva brought up the subject of new relationships in class, she started a lively discussion. Everyone was vitally interested in opening Pandora's Box.

Whether a particular divorced person *should* marry or not is a decision that *the individual* must make based on his or her own situation and God's word. Every divorced single, however, needs improved relationship tools. He must evaluate his own strengths, weaknesses and patterns of relating to other people in order to restore his self-confidence and rebuild self-esteem as he moves toward divorce recovery.

Jed's reply to Geneva was, "I've learned from my mistakes, too, but not enough. I don't want to get married. Every time I get to know a woman, I think she's just like my wife, and I know that didn't work. I don't want a repeat performance. You'd all jump down my throat if I said, 'All women are alike'; so I won't say that.

"Instead I'll ask, 'Why is it that I keep discovering the same type over and over?' I meet a woman, and I think she's great or interesting or fascinating, then I get to know her better, and I discover she has the same problems my wife and others have. They are all martyrs, and I don't want that."

The class probed Jed for more information. Many in class identified their tendency to also have repeating patterns, just as Jed did.

PATTERNS IN RELATIONSHIPS

Patterns do exist in relationships, and they tend to repeat. The trick is to recognize your pattern of relating and change it, or else you enter new relationships with old tools.

As Jed talked on, his pattern became more evident when he said, "I pay attention to a woman's eyes. I suppose I could say the same kind of eyes always attracts me. The women are different though, but there is a similarity in eyes. Well, maybe the women are not too different though, since I said they all end up being alike by being martyrs. But I start out thinking each one is different. I'm really getting confused."

After listening to Jed a bit more, Alicia said, "Jed, I think you're a sucker for sad-eyed women. It seems to me that you key in on the sad eyes, and then you discover that they are really sad women. Was you wife sad-eyed, too?"

"Yeah, she was. I'm going to have to think about this. I believe you hit on something there."

We went on to identify the patterns that keep repeating.

Dependent/Rescuer

Dependency was one of the patterns that kept coming up in the discussion. Dependency and rescuer match up, so it seemed, but not for a healthy relationship.

The dependent person can be a person who leans heavily on someone else for strength. The rescuer is the one who wants to provide that strength. Often the alcoholic is a dependent person, for instance. A rescuer wants to save the alcoholic from self-destruction. So, these two match up in order for each to play out his role.

Alcoholics Anonymous says the worst thing you can do for alcoholics is rescue them from the consequences of their dependency. If they are continually rescued, they never give up their dependency.

The same is true of people who have the emotional dependency disease. They must learn to face their dependency in order to overcome it.

The rescuer bounces from one dependent person to another, and each relationship fails because one person cannot provide all the strength for both. The dependent person keeps looking outside self for strength, instead of developing personal strength.

If the rescuer succeeds, his role is no longer needed, and the relationship ends. The pattern repeats for both and fails for both.

Master/Slave

Regina confessed a pattern in her relationships, too. "I am so strong-willed that I think I need a man who is stronger for me to respect him. So, I get involved with someone I think is stronger, and it turns out he thinks he is lord and master, and he expects me to be his slave. That isn't what I wanted. I don't want the 'me Tarzan, you Jane' scene. But that's what I get into. So, my relationships end with Tarzan swinging over to the other side of the river because I don't make a good Jane."

While it's more often a male-master/woman-slave problem, sometimes the roles are reversed to woman-master/male-slave. Neither of these patterns is a biblical one. Neither pattern works.

God did not intend for one person to be lord and master over another, whether male or female. It is Christ who is Lord and Master of the universe, and he is Lord of love and Master of compassion. We are simply partners in his service, no more and no less.

Martyr/Nurturer

By now Jed was putting pieces of his puzzle together. "Regina, your master/slave pattern is similar to my situation. You keep looking for a particular characteristic, even though that doesn't work. That's what I'm doing. I keep going to the sad eyes, a particular characteristic. I am a nurturer, and I keep responding to the women who are martyrs and want nurturing. But then I get tired of too much need in them, and I walk away. I can see an unhealthy pattern here. I need to change it, quickly."

Jed's right, of course. The martyr has the "I gave up everything for this relationship," sad-eyed, Joan of Arc attitude. This forces the nurturer into the position of always having to try and keep the martyr happy about being in the relationship. This may manifest itself in flowers, candy, extravagant gifts, gushy notes, etc.

None of this works, though, because the problem is *within* the martyr and cannot be salved away with chocolate ointment. Instead, it takes an internal dose of castor oil to the attitude to elicit a remedy.

CHANGE PATTERNS

Recognizing the unhealthy pattern is the first step in changing it. The second step is to develop new tools. Everyone had a quick, easy answer for Jed.

"Jed, quit being suckered by sad eyes. Look for sparkly eyes. Or quit looking at eyes, and look at the whole person. Quit keying in on one characteristic. That's not realistic."

This was a new tool for Jed. He resolved to get a new yardstick. His old yardstick wasn't measuring as accurately as he needed it to.

What You See May Not Be What You Get

Being realistic is also a new tool to take into relationships. Two people meet. Each puts his best foot forward and the fairy tale begins. Strained images are hard to hold on to, so each person eventually reverts to being his real self. It's so much easier to be real, to be authentic, at all times. Then there isn't the worry of maintaining an image. The authentic you attracts an authentic other.

To be authentic, practice showing your emotional self. Express your real thoughts and feelings, instead of just 'going along.' Listen, watch and learn. This is realistic.

Realistic Expectations

As you are more realistic in behavior, get your expectations on a realistic level, too. It's realistic to expect sad-eyed people to have sad dispositions. It's unrealistic to think you can rescue them. You might inspire someone to rescue himself, but if a relationship is built on this only, once someone is rescued, you're out of a job. So you have to maintain the dependency to be needed, or look for another job.

To have realistic expectations, know that the real purposes of marriage are to help each other get to heaven, to share life with a person and to add to the other's life. It is not to receive happiness from someone, or for someone to fill your life's bucket. Those things come from within *you*.

It's unrealistic to expect marriage to make you whole, make you happy, or to think those special feelings are a strong foundation for marriage. Feelings change. You know that now, don't you?

In developing realistic expectations it's helpful to know that discontent with *others* is most often discontent with *self*. To keep from being disappointed by others, build up the contentment level within yourself. Build up your self-esteem, your acceptance of self and your acceptance of your situation. This will go a long way in breaking patterns in relationships that are unhealthy.

As our discussion continued, Jed asked, "Why do I keep going for the sad eyes? I know it isn't what I want for a long term."

Geneva tossed out this idea. "Could it be since you said your wife also was sad-eyed, and your marriage failed, that you are trying to prove that you can succeed in the same circumstances?"

An "aha" expression showed on Jed's face. He looked as though he were saying, "That's it! That's the key I've been looking for." A quiet hush fell over the group as everyone applied this thought personally.

It's true. Too often we repeat patterns to try to prove we can succeed in the same circumstance. To break the pattern and develop realistic expectations, give up this need to prove you can do it. That circumstance is finished. A new and different pattern, a realistic circumstance will be more satisfying.

As this class ended, Jed and Regina agreed to take a close look at their patterns and how to break them in the future. Since the topic of relationships is so vital to divorcees, the next week's class was a continuation with Jed opening the discussion.

PURPOSE OF RELATIONSHIPS

"I've thought all week about my patterns in relationships. I can see that I've been trying to prove that I'm not a failure. I felt like such a failure right after the divorce. My self-esteem was right down on the ground.

"I can also see that I set myself up for disappointment by having unrealistic expectations. I can change this and develop better relationships in the future.

"But, unlike Geneva, I still don't want to get married. Sure, I get lonely, and I want companionship, but does it have to lead to marriage? I don't want everyone I date to evaluate me as a potential marriage partner. And I'd like to enjoy dating without the threat of getting hooked. Is this an unreal expectation?"

Wow! Another Pandora's Box. Before we could answer that, Geneva asked, "If I don't consider each man I date as a potential husband, then what's the purpose in dating? What's it for?"

Ideas and opinions flew around the room. We listed the answers. Some were out in left field, such as, "So I will know my phone hasn't been disconnected" and "To give me a reason for using mouthwash."

Practice Relating

One of the right-field purposes for dating was expressed as practice in relating. We obviously were a group who needed practice. Nobody has had too much practice in relating to others. Instead of evaluating every person of the opposite sex as a potential mate, it was concluded it might be good to look at them as a learning experience.

This approach makes each person an exciting adventure, someone from whom you can learn more than you knew before. You can learn more about others and more about yourself, too.

Build Friendships

It was decided that another purpose for dating is to develop friendships. Friendships are very important. Nobody has too many friends. Friendships add a great deal of satisfaction to life because we are people persons.

Friendships are built by listening and listening, and talking. In friendships you deal with reality, the real you. The real you expresses, "These are my weaknesses," and "These are my strengths," "This is something you need to know about me," and "This is something maybe you can help me with."

To get to know others, you build friendships because people need people. You plug in to people by relating to them. Jed was expressing this need when he said he wanted companionship. People put us back together again. Dr. Paul Faulkner expressed this well when he said, "There are no happy hermits."

Since people need people, all relationships are meaningful when built on friendship. Building friendships takes time and practice and responsibility.

Responsibility. Friendships carry a responsibility of commitment. As your friend I am committed to considering your welfare and your feelings. As your friend, I am committed to not walking out if the going gets tough.

Commitment. Friendship is a commitment to being there in time of need.

Tedd and Neil are my friends. I can call them and say, "I am so upset." They respond appropriately with, "What are you upset about?" They don't say, "You're interrupting my work on a crossword puzzle. Later."

I can also call Tedd and Neil and say, "I'm so excited! Wait 'til you hear my good news." They again respond appropriately with, "Tell me. Tell me." They don't say, "I'm watching 'The Cosby Show' right now. Later."

I can depend on their being there because friendships share the good and the bad.

Communication. Friendships also carry a responsibility of communication, honest communication, the communication of the ups and downs of life. We all want that level of communication that says, "I can tell you anything — I can reveal my imperfections and not be laughed at or scorned." As friends you communicate acceptance, of the real you and of the real other.

Confirmation. As friends we confirm each other. Give that "You're okay" affirmation that everyone needs and wants. Nourish and feed relationships so people can say, "I'm glad I know you."

THE APPLE TREE

It all boils down to reinvesting yourself in people. Taking the risk again. Reaching out again. It reminds me of when I was a tomboy kid back home. We had this old apple tree that we climbed in the back yard. Every spring that old tree blossomed out in gorgeous white blooms, and by summer it was loaded down with big, red apples. All the kids in the neighborhood knew they were welcome to take an apple and eat it; so, there were kids in that tree every day.

There was only one problem. The apples grew out on the ends of the branches, and because the tree was older and taller, the branches were too high to reach from the ground for us kids. That meant we had to climb up the tree and edge out toward the end of the branches to get the apples. The farther you went toward the fruit, the more limber the branches were. Sometimes you really had to weigh the risk of the limb's breaking against the juicy, sweet taste of that fruit to decide if you were willing to edge your way on out or not. Most of the time we went for the fruit, and the limb was stronger than we thought.

That's how relationships work. You have to weigh the risk against the sweet fellowship of friendship. You have to edge your way out toward the fruit of life, take the risk, reach out and take hold of the sweetness. It can't come to you; you have to go get it. Sure, it's a little precarious sometimes. It makes you nervous and unsure sometimes, especially when you've had a branch break beneath you before and you fell to the ground. But it's worth it to try again.

Remember that when you fall off a horse, the best thing to do is get up and ride again to overcome the fear. And, if you break your leg, you have to let it heal and then start walking again. You don't want to be an invalid all your life. Nor do you want to be an emotional or social invalid because you were once broken by a relationship. You have to get up and go for it again. You have to climb back up in the apple tree and begin inching your way out toward the fruit. When you get to the sweet fellowship, you'll find that it's good right down to the last bite.

CELEBRATION OF GRACE

Jed was satisfied with the discussion on relationships. "I have learned some of what I needed to know to make future relationships better. At least I see my pattern, and I feel I'm not unrealistic in thinking that I want friendships, without wanting to get married. I want the option of changing my mind; but right now, I've got too much to learn about relating well. Marriage isn't always the answer. After all, remember, turkeys flock. Eagles soar solo!"

Jed's right. Being single is not a state of premarried or postmortem. It's not the unfortunate residue of the unmarried. It's a life of freedom and choices in Christ. It's a life of love, hope and joy. It's a productive life of service to God and his children. It's part of the sweet fruit of life. It's a celebration of the grace of God.

Divorce Recovery Journal

To help you learn more about relating well, get out your divorce recovery journal and write about the similarities in your relationships.

This relationship business is so important that you need to also think and write about what you really want in a relationship.

Besides the relationship, think about the person. Write about the kind of people you really like.

Then complete these statements:

1. When I really feel good about another person, I feel . . .

2. My weaknesses and strengths in relationships are . . .

BIBLIOGRAPHY

Besson, Clyde. *Picking Up the Pieces*. New York: Ballantine Books, 1982.

Faulkner, Paul. *Making Things Right, When Things Go Wrong*. Fort Worth, TX: Sweet Publishing, 1986.

Fisher, Bruce. *Rebuilding*. San Luis Obispo, CA: Impact Publishers, 1981.

Harley, Willard F. Jr. *His Needs Her Needs*. Old Tappan, NJ: Fleming H. Revell Co., n.d.

McKay, Matthew. *The Divorce Book*. Oakland, CA: New Harbinger Publications, 1984.

Smoke, Jim. *Growing Through Divorce*. Eugene, OR: Harvest House, 1985.

Small Group Study Guide

by Mike Washburn

About the Author

This Leader's Guide has been written and prepared by Mike Washburn. Mike is the highly respected singles' minister for a 600-member singles' program in a large church in Fort Worth, Texas. He holds the Bachelor of Arts in Religion and the Master of Arts in New Testament Studies.

Mike is in constant demand as a resource speaker for singles' workshops and seminars nationwide. He serves as coordinator and host of the National Singles' Retreat and the annual Single Again National Retreat. He is also a featured speaker at the semiannual Church Growth Workshop, helping churches nationwide to develop and build successful singles' programs. The Divorce Recovery program has been instituted and developed under his direction.

Mike is the Executive Editor of *Single Today*, a national newsletter for singles. He has previously published articles in *20th Century Christian*, *Single Source*, *Single Again*, *TEACH Newsletter* and *Single Today*.

Mike and his wife Sharon have served in a singles' ministry since 1980. They have two daughters, Randi and Taylor.

Introduction

When I was twenty-one years old, my wife died from cancer. I was not prepared for her death, nor did I want to be single-again. Losing her in that way was the toughest thing I had ever faced. However, that experience paled in comparison to the struggle of putting my life back together with no support group. I made mistakes and felt horribly negative emotions. And no one was there to assure me that it's okay to fail or that the negative emotions are normal. My recovery process was slowed and complicated because I did not find a supportive group who understood my situation.

Because of my experience, I determined I would do all I could to see that others did not duplicate my experience of non-support. So, in 1980 as a singles' minister in Houston, Texas, I began by trial and error, a support group for those needing recovery from divorce. I have made many mistakes through the years but have learned a lot, too. I hope what I have learned will benefit you in your ministry.

Guidelines

A. *Divorce Recovery* needs to be used in a "support group" setting. A support group differs from a typical class in a number of ways:

1) The support group does not have a teacher per se, but it has facilitators who work together creating an experience as opposed to imparting information.

2) Dispensing information is not the goal; rather, it is allowing each person to have a cathartic experience working through the various topics of discussion.

3) Finishing the lesson is not the main objective, but addressing the needs of the people where they are is of utmost importance. Don't get agenda anxiety if the group feels the need to go in a different direction than your lesson plan.

4) It is relationships and the support they give which will give long-term help in the recovery process. Help create fellowship opportunities.

B. Begin and end each session in exactly the same way. Stability is of prime importance for those whose lives are in turmoil.

1) Begin by welcoming everyone and introducing all newcomers.

2) Ask each newcomer to tell how they found out about the group and to share a little bit about themselves. Don't be surprised by what you hear, and take as long as needed.

3) List the rules:

a) No one has to talk if he doesn't want to.

b) *Nothing* will be repeated outside the support group itself.

4) Ask if anyone has anything he would like to share from the past week's experiences.

5) Ask if anyone would like to share any new insights learned from his personal divorce recovery journal that is a part of each chapter of this book.

6) Introduce the topic to be discussed, followed by lesson questions.

7) Always end with affirmation time and prayer, allowing approximately five minutes for this.

C. Because divorce causes negative emotions, do not be surprised by what you hear. Remember, this is a support group, not a judgment group.

Feelings are neither good nor bad. If negative feelings are ever going to heal, they must be acknowledged and then dealt with. Suppression doesn't help anyone, nor does hearing someone say, "Oh, you must not feel that way." Remember, love is the great healer, and love is patient.

D. Allow the group members themselves to discover the answers to the dilemmas they face. Don't supply all the answers for them. As a leader of the support group, you should not march them through the battlefield like a general, but you are to lead them gently toward recovery as a shepherd leads his sheep to cool waters and greener pastures.

SESSION 1:
A ROLLER COASTER RIDE
(The Process of Divorce)

Text: Romans 5:1-8

Change is at the heart of God's plan for every person. It is his desire that everyone change, improve, and grow as an individual. However, growth is sidestepped by not dealing properly with the truth – by denying that change is necessary. Only by owning our own past failures can we create a better future.

Session Goals/Objectives:

1. Realize that denial is a coping mechanism for the trauma of divorce.
2. Divorce does not make you half a person. The only role lost is the role of husband/wife.
3. Help participants realize that they must deal with many myths concerning divorce and that these are normal and must be set aside.

Discussion Starters:

1. Denial, as a coping mechanism, is played out in many ways:
  - Drinking yourself into oblivion.
  - Sleeping an exaggerated number of hours.
  - Fantasizing the marriage as being wonderful, with no memory of the bad times in the relationship.
Ask volunteer group members to share what forms of denial they used to cope with the initial stage of shock that comes from a failed marriage.
2. Say, "Jesus said in John 8:32, 'You shall know the truth and the truth will set you free.' How does facing the truth about your divorce set you free?"
3. Following the "owning of denial" by group members, have them share experiences which helped them begin the healing transition.
4. List all the roles a person performs when married. Then list the roles performed after the marriage ends (i.e., everyone performs in the role of son or daughter). Allow several minutes for group members to complete the lists silently. Then, as a group, list the roles on the chalkboard. Identify the roles lost due to divorce. Question for discussion: "What lessons can be learned by this exercise?"

5. Say, "Share misconceptions you had about divorced people while you were still married."
6. Ask, "Now that your marriage has ended, what myths about divorce do you find yourself still believing?"
7. Say, "Anita stated, 'To get in control of life again, you need understanding, assurance, support and feelings of normalcy. Knowing that others have felt the same fears and uncertainties helps.' What have you heard in this session that has caused you to realize others feel many of the same feelings you do?"

SESSION 2:
THE UN-MERRY-GO-ROUND
(Dealing with Negative Emotions)

Text: Ephesians 4:26-27

Anger is a God-given emotion and should be appreciated as such. In its initial stages, anger energizes and motivates so that proper action can take place. However, anger that is harbored robs a person of vital energy and works against improving the situation.

Realize that Paul is giving a command to "be angry" in a way that results in positive action.

Session Goals/Objectives:

1. Help participants take ownership of their angry feelings.
2. Define God-given anger that motivates positive action verses self-destructive anger that enslaves and isolates the angered person from needed relationships.
3. Restore honor that has been, and is being, robbed by a controlling, self-destructive anger.

Discussion Starters:

1. Anger stems from frustration, fear and pain. Have each participant complete this sentence:
      "I always get angry when my ex-mate . . ."
2. Ask, "Do you knowingly do things that will prompt an angry response from your ex-mate? What?" Discuss.
3. Ask, "Does your being angry always mean your ex-mate is in control? Explain."
4. Say, "Explain how anger sometimes gains control for you and at other times gives control to your ex-mate."
5. Say, "Since transference of anger is a 'common occurrence,' share at least one humorous way you have taken out your anger at your ex-mate on someone or something else."
6. Say, "Since slashing tires and planting roadsigns in your ex-mate's yard are not acceptable means of behavior and do not restore honor, identify ways you have dealt successfully with anger from past hurts, frustrations and fears."

SESSION 3:
ALL HUNG UP
(Emotional Hang Ups)

Text: Philippians 3:13-14; 1 Corinthians 6:9-12

The way a person thinks translates into the way a person lives. The apostle Paul in Philippians 4:11-13 learned how to have a contented mind, even in difficult circumstances. In order for that to happen, he first had to apply the principle of thinking right things. After thinking right things (Philippians 4:8-9), a contented mind will follow. It is true that what a person sows in thought and deed is the very thing he will reap.

Session Goals/Objectives:

1. Help the group identify false beliefs that get in the way of their emotional health (e.g., "The divorce was all my fault!").
2. Have the group suggest positive, alternative thoughts to negative mindsets.
3. Help each person realize that everyone is a product of environment, as well as a product of choices he himself makes.

Discussion Starters:

1. Jim was an exceptional student, liked by his peers and a star athlete in high school. Then a diving accident left him paralyzed and drastically changed his life.

List on the board various attitudes Jim could have adopted following his accident.
2. Ask, "Since Jim had choices, what is the significance of the statement, 'We are products of our environment'?"
3. Ask, "Do you perceive that your situation has as many choices as Jim's, or are you frustrated by being a product of your environment more often than you'd like?"

On a sheet of paper, each person should honestly answer questions 4, 5 and 6. Follow this with group discussion of the answers given.
4. Ask, "Of the eight emotional hang ups described by Anita in chapter three, which one best describes you?"
5. Say, "List two examples you have role-played that cause you to fit the particular description."
6. Ask, "After having identified yourself, what alternative thought patterns could be used instead of the negative hang ups?"

Say, "List three alternative thought responses to these emotional hang ups." (During group discussion time, have the group explore additional alternative responses.)

REWIND, FAST FORWARD
OR EJECT
(Coming to Terms with the Past)

Text: 2 Corinthians 5:16-21

"A new creature" is what we are in Christ. Yet the thing that hinders most people from realizing full potential is the excess baggage we carry. You can't be a new creature while holding on to all your old mistakes and shortcomings. In Matthew 18:21, Peter asks the Lord, "How many times do I forgive?" Jesus responded with a parable about a slave who owed a lot of money to his master. At the same time, a fellow servant owed him a small amount of money. He asked pardon from his master concerning the large debt he owed, yet was unwilling to grant pardon for the small debt owed by his fellow servant.

The point of the parable is this: We have been pardoned as Christians from the large debt of sin against God; therefore, we are to emulate him and grant pardon to others who sin against us.

God is a forgiving being, and his forgiving nature allows all of us to continually have a "fresh start." The more we are like him, the more we will allow ourselves and others the chance for a new beginning. This can happen if we hear the words of Paul, when he says in Romans 12:3, "For by the grace given me I say to every one of you: Do not think of yourself more highly than you ought, but rather think of yourself with sober judgment, in accordance with the measure of faith God has given you."

Session Goals/Objectives:

1. Lead the group to realize that tendencies in dealing with the past are varied. Viewing past events in anger leads to exaggeration, and attempting to cope with past failures by downplaying events distorts what actually happened.
2. Help the group have a proper view of the past.
3. Work towards having group members accept their roles in past events.

Discussion Starters:

1. For this session you will need a prearranged role-playing argument. Choose two people to disagree, beginning an argument in

front of the unknowing group. Allow one to two minutes for this exchange. Upon completion, explain that the event was staged.

Now ask each group member to recall what he observed. Notice the differences in perspectives shared.

Talk about *why* events are viewed differently.

2. Make a group list of practical suggestions on how to gain a proper perspective of past events.

3. Ask, "Why is it when some of our 'memory tapes' are replayed they become more exaggerated than the actual event, while others are dismissed as unimportant?"

4. Have volunteers share one frequently-replayed "memory tape."

5. Have class members classify their perspectives as exaggerated, dismissed as unimportant, or factual.

6. With the help of the group, assist each person in finding the proper perspective of the shared "memory tape."

7. As a group, commit to filing the "memory tape" away, never to be replayed again.

SESSION 5:
FLASHBACKS
(Controlling Your Memories)

Text: Psalm 6

Grievers often think they are loosing their minds because of flashbacks and other similar memory experiences. Just when it is thought that a memory has been dealt with and resolved, it crops up again, throwing the griever off balance once again. If great care is not taken, the flashback experiences will have a negative impact for years to come. Flashbacks must be seen for what they are — a normal part of the grieving process, no more and no less.

Session Goals/Objectives:

1. Bring each member to the realization that flashback experiences are normal.
2. Help each group member develop a strategy for dealing properly with flashback experiences.
3. Teach participants not to take themselves too seriously, realizing the value of humor as it relates to past hurts.

Discussion Starters:

1. Ask each group member to share a flashback experience telling what resulted from it.
2. Identify any common threads of flashback reactions.
3. Ask, "What strategies can be used to resolve the irrational behavior resulting from flashbacks?"
4. Ask group members to take turns sharing their most embarrassing moments.
5. Ask, "What part does humor play in the healing process?"
6. Ask, "How can humor be used earlier to avoid embarrassment and additional hurts?"

SESSION 6:
THE DREAM ENDS
(Learning to Forgive)

Text: Psalm 51:1-4

Forgiveness may be the most difficult thing to fully accomplish in all of the recovery process. This is because so many things have taken place over long periods of time — hurts and wrongs involving any number of people, including self. The past can't be rewritten or undone, yet something must be done, or the past will continue to rear its ugly head at the most inopportune times. David was one who had much in his life that needed forgiveness, yet he was able to be a "man after God's own heart." If David was able to accomplish the transition from wrongs to forgiveness, we can, too.

Session Goals/Objectives:

1. Recognize the destructive nature of nonforgiveness.
2. Help group members own their part of the responsibility of the failed marriage, in order to begin forgiving self.
3. Help each person face the need to begin forgiving the ex-mate, and other persons if applicable.

Discussion Starters:

1. David was a main Old Testament character — he was a man after God's own heart. And, yet, he experienced many failures. As a group, list as many of these failures as you can.
2. Say, "David knew his failures, yet he was able to forgive himself. What are steps you can take to forgive yourself?"
3. On half the board make a list of reasons why *not* to forgive an ex-mate. On the other half of the board make a list of reasons why *to* forgive an ex-mate. After examining the two lists, discuss the reason or reasons it is hard to forgive an ex-mate.
4. Allow each participant time in class to write on three-by-five cards things about his ex-mate that need to be forgiven. Each card should contain only one event or trait needing forgiveness. Then, as each participant is able to forgive and let go of whatever has been written, he may tear the card up and throw the pieces away in a trash can in the middle of your circle. Others may not be able to forgive yet. These cards should be carried home with the goal of releasing one event at a time with forgiveness. Thus each card, one at a time, will be torn up and thrown away.

SESSION 7:
PLOP, PLOP, FIZZ, FIZZ
(Growth and Change)

Text: 1 John 4:18 Romans 12:1-2

If you're like me, then you like a routine — similar, pleasant experiences occurring over and over, day after day. Granted, some may call this a rut, and they may be right. But it's my rut, and I'm comfortable being in it.

Ruts do have their advantages. There is familiarity, which brings a certain amount of comfort. And there's a calmness knowing what event will come next in the routine.

On the other hand, ruts have their disadvantages. Being self-destructive in nature, ruts hinder growth. Part of the effort needed to change is spent "climbing out of the hole" created by sameness.

Ruts are lonely. After all, the rut is owned by you, which puts distance between you and others.

A third disadvantage to a rut is that reality is not taken into account. Life is ever changing, and if we are to live in the flow of life, we've got to change with it. We've got to get out of the rut.

Session Goals/Objectives:

1. Bring each group member to the realization that everyone has areas where change would benefit.
2. Help the group recognize things which hinder change.
3. Help each person learn that love conquers fear, enabling change to occur.

Discussion Starters:

1. Begin by reading the introductory paragraph to this session. Have group members share ruts they find themselves in and the disadvantages that result.
2. Ask, "Why do we dig ruts that eventually work against us and the people we'd like to become?"
3. Say, "Please make a list of all the character qualities you'd like to possess."
4. Then ask, "What keeps you from making the changes necessary to acquire those qualities?"
5. Ask, "Why is love the answer to casting out the fear which stifles change and growth?" (Read Romans 5:1-5.)
6. Have each group member commit to making one needed change in his/her life this week, in order to grow.

SESSION 8:

THE HOUSE OF HORRORS
(Coping with Your Former Spouse)

Text: Ephesians 5:31-32; Matthew 5:43-48

Dealing with the ex-mate can be one of the most confusing and difficult tasks of all the divorce processes. Not only is there a flood of emotions which confuse and complicate the encounters, but there is a wealth of history shared that must be but to rest.

Finding balance is the key to ending the intimate relationship on one hand, yet continuing "joint effort" with the children on the other. This is a juggling act that even the most skilled person has difficulty performing.

However, with proper understanding and follow-through, even the most difficult situations can be worked out.

Session Goals/Objectives:

1. Realize the importance of developing a workable strategy before encounters take place. This will not allow a "chance meeting" and shock value or set you back in your recovery.
2. Emphasize that even in this difficult dilemma of ending the intimacy while continuing a relationship with an ex-mate, each person is in charge and responsible for personal actions and emotions.
3. Help each person to give up feeling responsible for the welfare and happiness of the ex-mate.

Discussion Starters:

1. Put empty chairs between the participants at the beginning of the session. Ask, "If your ex-mates came into this session, how would your behavior be altered, and what emotions would be stirred up?"
2. Have each person share a "close encounter of the worst kind."
3. Ask each person to complete this sentence: "My biggest struggle in dealing with my ex-mate is . . ."
4. Ask, "Of the stages Anita describes in this chapter, which one presently describes you — vindictive, hostile, apathetic, relief or okay?"
5. Ask, "The washing machine of your ex-mate and the new 'live-in' breaks down. They come to you asking you to wash their dirty laundry. Would you do it? Why or why not?"

181

6. Ask, "Realizing how ridiculous the above situation is, under what circumstances would you be willing to help your ex-mate?"

7. On the board list as many constructive ways to deal with an ex-mate as the group can suggest.

SESSION 9:
THE FAMILY EXPRESS
(Coping with the Kids)

Text: Deuteronomy 6:6-7,20-24; Jeremiah 31:1; 1 Thessalonians 2:11

A Healthy Single-Parent Family . . .

. . . is made up of mentally healthy individuals who like and accept themselves, get along well with others, and cope successfully with life's problems.

. . . defines its basic purposes as protection, encouragement and love for all family members.

. . . sustains a supportive emotional environment.

. . . projects a positive, optimistic perspective and system of values.

. . . maintains effective patterns of communication.

. . . encourages a healthy balance between intimacy and autonomy.

. . . develops a responsible approach to resolving family problems.

. . . provides for flexible boundaries.

Achieving the healthy family state may take time, but it's good to know what goals to look toward and to know that with God's help all things are possible.

Session Goals/Objectives:

1. Identify potential problems for the children of divorce.
2. Identify potential needs for the single parent.
3. Encourage single parents in the Lord.

Discussion Starters:

1. Identify as many needs of the children of divorce as the group can.
2. Ask, "What are the major, felt needs of parents going through divorce as it relates to children?"
3. Ask, "Are there identifiably different problems for single fathers versus single mothers? What are the differences?"
4. Ask, "If you could tell a child of divorce anything, what would it be?" Have each person say one thing, making a list for all to see.
5. Ask, "If you could encourage a single parent in one way, what would you say?" Have each share verbally.

SESSION 10:
APPLYING THE S FORMULA
(Rebuilding Your Self-Esteem)

Text: Psalm 103:1-5; Psalm 139:1-17

There are times we all "get down" on ourselves, but it is an humbling thought to realize that God *never* "gets down" on us. His love is continual. He has shown us this by creating us in *his* image, then sacrificing his own son, so we can live with him forever.

The point of all of this cannot be missed. God thinks we're valuable, and he has not been wrong yet. The truth is, when someone else believes in you, it's a lot easier to believe in yourself.

God places value in each person, no matter what the past holds. God still highly esteems each one. Because of his esteem towards us, we should esteem ourselves in the same way.

Session Goals/Objectives:

1. Recognize that each divorcee is special, not because of what he is, but because of *whose* he is.
2. Help everyone understand that he has special qualities.
3. Help each person to find peace with the idea that it's all right to feel good about self.

Discussion Starters:

1. Ask each group member to complete these two statements: "When I feel bad about myself, it is because . . ." The thing that causes me to feel good about myself is . . ."
2. Two ways to love are: "because of" and "in spite of." On the board list the characteristics of both kinds of love.
3. God loves us with the highest form of love, "in spite of" love. Share with the group why it's hard to love self with "in spite of" love.
4. On separate three-by-five cards, have each person write down one good quality learned about every other person in the group. Have the group then focus on each person in the group one at a time, reading the positive qualities they have listed. When each person has been focused on, give them all the three-by-five cards containing their good qualities. Everyone is to keep his cards to review during "down" times or "blue Mondays."
5. For most people the receiving of verbalized compliments is not an easy thing to do. Have the group discuss this uncomfortable reaction, and why it is hard to receive compliments.

SESSION 11:
SEX: BLESSING OR BURDEN?
(Handling Your Sexuality as a Single)

Text: Genesis 2:18,25; Song of Solomon 2:7; 1 Corinthians 6:18-20

Society (and often Christians) has an image of single adults jumping from bed to bed, loving every minute of it, and it just isn't true. The "swinging single" doing anything and everything he or she wants without suffering any consequences is only a myth. The grass is not greener on the other side of the fence, and divorced singles will be the first to say so.

The problem is that physical desires don't die when the relationship does, and mistakes are sometimes made in attempting to find the right way to express those desires.

Thus, far too often, singles find themselves saying, like the apostle Paul, "For what I do is not the good I *want* to do; no, the evil I do not want to do, this I keep doing" (Romans 7:19).

Session Goals/Objectives:

1. Help the group identify true and false perceptions our society has about sexuality and singleness so that others' expectations will not affect their own behavior.
2. Help the group understand the destructive nature of using God's gift of sexuality in an incorrect way.
3. Immorality is a serious matter never to be taken lightly; however, it is not the unforgivable sin. Help each person own the forgiveness of God that is extended through Jesus Christ.

Discussion Starters:

1. Have the group make a list of perceptions married people in our society generally have about singleness and sex in America today. Write these on the board.
2. Of the list compiled, have the group decide which of the perceptions written on the board are false ones, telling why they are incorrect.
3. In 1 Corinthians 6:18, Paul talks about immorality being the one sin that is against one's own body. All other sins are outside the body. Discuss the significance of this verse.
4. List on the board as many negative consequences as the group can think of caused by using sexuality in the wrong ways.
5. If guilt, anger, further isolation and emotional confusion are the end products of sex without commitment, discuss what things

can be done to help bring the desires under control during the recovery process.

6. Realizing it is better to know personal limitations prior to temptation, have each person write on a three-by-five card his/her limits. This information should be kept private, given to much prayer concerning boundaries in one's life.

7. As the Divorce Recovery Facilitator, lead the entire group in a prayer, asking God to provide strength and comfort in this sensitive area.

8. Have the group discuss steps to take to get back on track when failures occur.

SESSION 12:
TOO GUARDED TO LOVE
(Establishing Trust and Love Again)

Text: 2 Chronicles 20:20; Isaiah 26:4

When you lose the ability to trust, it leaves a house full of unwanted guests. The inability to trust others equals isolation and eventual loneliness. Without the capacity to trust God, you are left faithless. When you cease to trust yourself, the result is low self-esteem, leading to depression. And, if you lose the ability to trust in life itself, the by-product is cynicism.

No one should be one hundred percent trusting of everyone and everything, because that person would be what the Proverbs describe as a simpleton. Nor should a person allow cynicism, caused by a lack of trust, to rule either. So the struggle is present for each one to find his own level of trust in every situation in life.

There is one area in each of our lives, however, where we should be striving to be one hundred percent trusting. This area is our relationship with God. It is not easy nor instant, but as we grow in trust in a perfect God, it becomes easier to cope with imperfection, including others and self.

Session Goals/Objectives:

1. Identify for the group the importance of establishing a trusting relationship with the Lord first and foremost.
2. Help each person identify the amount of trust he is putting in others.
3. Focus on ways to become more trusting.

Discussion Starters:

1. Say, "Psalm 118:8 says, 'It is better to take refuge in the Lord than to trust in men.' Why is that so?"
2. Ask, "What effects should our conclusions about question number one have on our relationships with others? Can we ever trust others? If so, how?"
3. List behavioral characteristics that are evident in a person stuck in a nontrusting mode in relationships.

4. On a one-to-ten scale, with one being "completely nontrusting" and ten being "completely trusting," have class members identify their positions on the scale. Explore why they have chosen a particular number on the scale.

5. Ask, "Can a person ever overcome the inability to trust?"

6. Have volunteers share ways they have or think they can overcome the inability to trust.

SESSION 13:
OPENING PANDORA'S BOX
(Facing New Relationships)

Text: Matthew 5:43-48; James 3:13-18; Romans 12:9-21

Relationships are among those things you can't live without but at times are hard to live with as well. They can bring the greatest joys life has to offer or the world's greatest sorrows.

Anytime the potential for joy and sorrow are this great in regard to relationships, it emphasizes the great care needed in structuring them properly.

The one-flesh relationship between husband and wife does not happen instantly, but instead is a life-long pursuit.

Many things hinder healthy relationships, both in their creation and their continuation. However, healthy, satisfying relationships are formed with great care and the enabling power of God.

Session Goals/Objectives:

1. Help each person discover his/her capacity to create healthy relationships.
2. Help each person to understand things that hinder the development of a healthy relationship.
3. Establish that a healthy, satisfying relationship is possible for each person, *if* certain responsibilities are owned by that person.

Discussion Starters:

1. Have each person make a list of characteristics describing an ideal relationship. Have each one share the list verbally with the class.
2. Ask group members to make another list describing the characteristics that lead to their last failed dating relationships or failed marriages (e.g., poor communication, etc.).
3. Say, "Please finish this sentence: 'Dating in today's society is difficult because . . .' "
4. Say, "Anita said, 'Patterns of relationships tend to repeat themselves.' If you are able, identify your own patterns of relating to this group."
5. Make a list on half the board of the reasons for marriage. On the other half of the board, list the reasons not to marry.
6. Ask each person to fill in this blank: "In my next relationship, I commit to do _____ differently."

RECOMMENDED RESOURCES

Marriage and Remarriage

Adams, Jay E. *Marriage Divorce & Remarriage*. Phillipsburg, NJ; Presbyterian and Reformed Publishing Company, 1980.

Bales, James D., *Not Under Bondage*. Searcy, AR; James D. Bales Publishing, 1979.

Richards, Larry. *Remarriage, a Healing Gift from God*. Waco, TX; Word Incorporated, 1981.

Woodroff, James S. *The Divorce Dilemma*. Nashville, TN; Christian Family Books, 1977.

Relationships

Augsburger, David. *Caring Enough to Confront*. Ventura, CA; Regal Books, 1983.

Augsburger, David. *Caring Enough to Forgive*. Ventura, CA; Regal Books, 1981.

Augsburger, David. *Caring Enough to Hear*. Ventura, CA; Regal Books, 1981.

Augsburger, David. *When Caring is not Enough*. Ventura, CA; Regal Books, 1983.

Getz, Gene A. *Loving One Another*. Wheaton, IL; Victor Books, 1979.

McGinnis, Alan Loy. *The Friendship Factor*. Minneapolis; Augsburg Publishing House, 1979.

Wright, Norman. *An Answer to Loneliness*. Irvine, CA; Harvest House Publishing, 1977.

Singles and Sex

Beauchamp, Gary R. *God Loves the Single, Too*, Nashville, TN; The Christian Teacher, Inc., 1978.

Dillow, Joseph. *Solomon on Sex*. Nashville, TN; Thomas Nelson, Inc., 1977.

Miles, Herbert J. *Singles, Sex and Marriage*. Waco, TX; Word Books, 1983.

Pettus Robert L. Jr., M.D. *As I See Sex Through the Bible*. Nashville, TN; Williams, 1973.

Smedes, Lewis B. *Sex for Christians*. Grand Rapids, MI; William B. Eerdmans Publishing Co., 1980.

General

Buscaglia, Leo, Ph.D. *Living, Loving & Learning*. New York; Ballantine Books, 1982.

Dobson, James, Dr. *Emotions — Can You Trust Them?*. Ventura, CA; Regal Books, 1980.

Durham, Ken, Dr. *Speaking from the Heart*. Fort Worth, TX; Sweet Publishing, 1986.

Faulkner, Paul, Dr. *Making Things Right, When Things Go Wrong*. Fort Worth, TX; Sweet Publishing, 1986.

Divorce Recovery

Allen, Charles L. *When a Marriage Ends*. Old Tappan, NJ; 1986.

Hensley, J. Clark. *Coping with Being Single Again*. Nashville, TN; Broadman Press, 1978.

May, Bernie. *Learning to Trust*. Portland, OR; Multnomah Press, 1985.

McKay, Matthew, Ph.D.; Pogers, Peter, Ph.D.; Blades, Joan, J.D.; Gosse, Richard, M.A., *The Divorce Book*. Edited by Kirk & Susan Johnson. Oakland, CA; New Harbinger Publishing, 1984.

Rambo, Lewis R. *The Divorcing Christian*. Nashville, TN; Abingdon Press, 1984.